Departures

Critical Refugee Studies

EDITED BY THE CRITICAL REFUGEE STUDIES COLLECTIVE

Departures

AN INTRODUCTION TO CRITICAL
REFUGEE STUDIES

The Critical Refugee Studies Collective

Yến Lê Espiritu | Lan Duong | Ma Vang | Victor Bascara
Khatharya Um | Lila Sharif | Nigel Hatton

UNIVERSITY OF CALIFORNIA PRESS

University of California Press
Oakland, California

© 2022 by Yến Lê Espiritu and Lan Duong

About the cover art: Priscilla Otani's installation *Our Hearts Beat As One* represents the shared desire of migrants for survival and regeneration. The paper umbrella represents a fragile shelter, a destination reached, though not as secure as expected. The inside spokes provide a narrow perch where the travelers cluster to stay warm. The fallen leaves beneath the umbrella offer both sustenance and a burial ground. The wings falling from the umbrella convey tears at the fleetingness of life.

Library of Congress Cataloging-in-Publication Data

Names: Espiritu, Yen Le, 1963- author. | Duong, Lan P., 1972- author. | Vang, Ma, 1982- author. | Bascara, Victor, 1970- author. | Um, Khatharya, author. | Sharif, Lila, 1984- author. | Hatton, Nigel, 1973- author.
Title: Departures : an introduction to critical refugee studies / Yến Lê Espiritu, Lan Duong, Ma Vang, Victor Bascara, Khatharya Um, Lila Sharif, Nigel Hatton.
Other titles: Critical refugee studies ; 3.
Description: Oakland, California : University of California Press, [2022] | Series: Critical refugee studies ; 3 | Includes bibliographical references and index.
Identifiers: LCCN 2022004935 (print) | LCCN 2022004936 (ebook) | ISBN 9780520386365 (cloth) | ISBN 9780520386389 (paperback) | ISBN 9780520386396 (ebook)
Subjects: LCSH: Refugees—Government policy—United States. | Refugees—Legal status, laws, etc.—United States. | Immigrants—Government policy—United States. | Asylum, Right of—United States.
Classification: LCC JV6601 .E76 2022 (print) | LCC JV6601 (ebook) | DDC 323.6/31—dc23/eng/20220520
LC record available at https://lccn.loc.gov/2022004935
LC ebook record available at https://lccn.loc.gov/2022004936

31 30 29 28 27 26 25 24 23 22
10 9 8 7 6 5 4 3 2 1

This book is dedicated to every human being who is affected by displacement

Contents

Acknowledgments

We are here because you were there. This aphorism, coined by the London-based Sri Lankan political essayist Ambalavaner Sivanandan, captures with elegant simplicity the colonial and imperialist legacies of migration. Focusing on refugee lives, this book advances Sivanandan's core argument: forced migrations don't just happen; they are produced.

But in acknowledgment of those who came before us, those who walk beside us, and those who will follow us, we imbue Sivanandan's phrase with new meaning—that we are *here* because *you* were there:

You, our families, whose stories and histories incite our work
You, our communities, whose actions and wisdoms inform our
    praxis
You, our colleagues, whose brilliance and boldness influence our
    writing
You, our students, whose dreams and passion inspire our vision

We also thank the University of California Humanities Research Institute (UCHRI) and the University of California Office of the

President (UCOP) for funding what became the Critical Refugee Studies Collective and Naomi Schneider and Summer Farah at the University of California Press for supporting this book project and the Critical Refugee Studies book series.

Thank you all for helping us get *here*. This book is for you, for us. *We are here because you were there.*

Prologue

A Letter to Our Communities

Writing in a Time of Crises

This book is for our communities. It was written in the midst of mass population displacement. In 2020, over 70 million asylum seekers, refugees, and stateless people were forced out of their homes worldwide; in essence, every two seconds, one person is forcibly displaced somewhere in the world.[1] As the Pulitzer Prize–winning author Viet Thanh Nguyen reminds us, if refugees formed their own country, it would be the world's twenty-fourth largest—bigger than South Africa, Spain, Iraq, or Canada.[2] Closer to home, closer to our communities, these statistics signal to us a political mode of cruelty that has been emboldened and inflamed by Trumpism in recent years. At the same time, we have always known that the US government has been guided by xenophobic and racist immigration policies, even as such policies are cloaked in the rhetoric of neoliberal concern and tolerance. The policies that defined President Trump's tenure—denying entry to immigrants from Muslim-majority countries, caging children at the borders, forcing hysterectomies on Latinx women, and separating asylum-seeking families—have only clarified for us the logics of white supremacy and operations of racial capitalism underlying US empire and its expansion. The refusal to accept refugees on the part of many Western countries is a contagion, founded in a Westphalian attachment to sovereignty, and in the United States it is becoming increasingly virulent in the militarization at the border. Even more distressingly, the politics of the pandemic have intersected with xenophobia, in that refugees have been detained at the US-Mexico border due to Title 42, an obscure public health policy that illegally and without due process turns away migrants who are deemed health threats. This course of action was promulgated by Trump with respect to Central American migrants and is now being extended to Haitians by President Joe Biden because of COVID-19. Reminiscent of the laws barring Asians from entering the United States in the late nineteenth century, Title 42 currently allows Biden to detain and expel Haitians, who, after experiencing the assassination of President Joivenel Moïse, a 7.2 magnitude earthquake, and a disastrous flood storm in the last six months of 2020, have fled their country and traveled to Mexico to apply for asylum in the United States.[3]

During the time of this writing, we also find ourselves in the midst of a global pandemic and the Black Lives Matter (BLM) uprisings.[4] In July 2021, the US COVID-19 death toll topped 610,000 and has continued to climb.[5] Confirmed COVID-19 cases and deaths are disproportionately higher in African American, Latinx,[6] and Indigenous communities,[7] as they are the most vulnerable populations who make up the bulk of the "essential workers" needed to ensure the safety and well-being of the privileged classes and who have little access to affordable healthcare. Asian Americans, especially Filipino Americans and Pacific Islanders, are also fatally impacted by the virus because of their occupations as nurses and caregivers[8] and because of predisposed conditions like hypertension, high cholesterol, and diabetes.[9] It is clear that these populations were already made vulnerable to illness because of systemic and social inequities: "higher levels of poverty; crowded housing; [and] multigenerational households [that] make it more difficult to physically distance or quarantine."[10] A discourse about imperial power and the audacity of US exceptionalism underlies media reports on the virus. At one point, we were told that it is wartime, that the virus was an invisible foreign enemy, and that the death toll had exceeded the number of Americans who died during the Vietnam War.[11] Such militarized, jingoistic discourse is meant to evoke the notion of collective sacrifice and national victories. But at its core, we know that the coronavirus, what Iyko Day calls the "great revealer," has exposed the vast structural inequalities that racial capitalism continues to reproduce and that neoliberalism has sharpened at the expense of human lives and the environment.[12]

Systemic violence and social inequities have also fueled the BLM protest movement, considered the "largest movement in U.S. history."[13] George Floyd, who was brutally murdered at the hands of the Minneapolis police, inspired an estimated 15 to 26 million people to rise up against a white supremacist police state and demand a future beyond police violence.[14] The protesters demand justice not only for George Floyd but also for the many other African American men and women (or those who identify as such) and children, including Ahmaud Arbery, Breonna Taylor, Eric Garner, Rayshard Brooks, Philando Castile, Atatiana Jefferson, and Tamir Rice, who have been killed by police. Demonstrations against police brutality and racism were also organized worldwide—in South Korea, Japan, Jamaica, Canada, Australia, Hong Kong,

England, France, Belgium, Germany, Brazil, the Netherlands, Nairobi, and the West Bank.[15] For us, protesters who continue to demonstrate against police brutality are among the "essential" ones, as they stand at the front lines of a vast political movement for social justice. That these killings and other injustices are occurring within the same time frame underscores their interconnectedness through the logic of racial capitalism, a calculus in which, as Ruth Wilson Gilmore puts it, "capitalism requires inequality and racism enshrines it."[16] Add to it the deleterious effects of the pandemic, and this formula becomes deadly for Black, Indigenous, and People of Color (BIPOC), as "racism and capitalism mutually construct harmful social conditions that fundamentally shape COVID-19 disease inequities."[17] This confirms what we already know—that such inequities for BIPOC people in the United States are historically and systemically linked to "segregation, homelessness, medical bias," and lack of access to healthcare.[18]

During the COVID-19 pandemic and the BLM rebellions, refugees have intermittently appeared and disappeared in the US media. On the one hand, refugees are an unknown in the drive to contain COVID-19: the data on refugees and COVID-19 in the global context remain scant, due in large part to the lack of testing.[19] On the other hand, a refugee, Tou Thao, a Hmong American police officer who stood guard while his fellow officer murdered Floyd, figures prominently in Floyd's killing. As Ma Vang and Kit Myers write, the larger context for Thao's complicity is a troubling continuity of his form of "soldiering,"[20] one that links the wars in Southeast Asia to the urban setting of Minneapolis, in which "[his] recruitment and work as a Minneapolis police officer is consistent with U.S. imperialist practices to recruit Hmong as proxy soldiers during the 'secret war.'"[21]

We Need a New Analytic

As refugees are nowhere and everywhere, we need a new analytic. *Departures: An Introduction to Critical Refugee Studies* places refugees at the fulcrum of the intersecting discourses of militarism and war, migration and resettlement, and displacement and dispossession that continue to structure our past and present. The latest example is the collapse of the US-backed Afghan government in August 2021, two decades after US-led forces toppled the Taliban regime in what became the United States's longest war, which resulted in the displacement of vast numbers of Afghans, who already make up the largest protracted refugee population in Asia and the second largest refugee population in the world. We make the case that refugees and the issue of displacement must be front and center in the ways we talk about the deleterious effects of climate change, global epidemics, and perpetual war. We also insist that the genocide of Native Americans and the enslavement of African Americans have predisposed the United States to a deeply ingrained white supremacist culture. As such, it is impossible to think through refugeehood without also reflecting on "the willing amnesia of settler colonialism," as Leti Volpp argues,[22] since refugee policies and immigration laws surrounding sovereignty and the foreigner involve a presupposition about a nation-state's territories and borders, a premise that "relies tacitly on the dispossession of already existing populations."[23] The question of slavery also brings to bear the painful notion that Black bodies, marked as fugitive and fungible, have been forcibly moved and trafficked across borders for more than four hundred years. Accordingly, Black refugee flight can be traced to countries like Canada, the United States, Haiti, Nova Scotia, and others in centuries past and most resoundingly today. In the contemporary United States, Black people are a growing segment of the immigrant population who pass through US borders, and it is here that "more than [any] other immigrant group, undocumented black foreign-born people find themselves caught in the prison to deportation pipeline."[24]

That these borders, as vestiges of colonial violence, have an increasingly militarized presence today speaks directly to the over-militarized policing of BIPOC people in US cities. Seeking to protect property above and beyond humans, an enactment that is a direct descendant of chattel slavery and its history, police forces are heavily armed with weaponry that snakes across the country after having been deployed in the perpetual wars waged overseas by the United States. Our focus on settler colonialism is deliberate and dovetails well with the processes of re/settlement that refugees undergo in moving, and in being forced to move, from place to place, a phenomenon described by Eric Tang as an "unending state of arrival at liberalism," in the supposed land of salvation that is the United States.[25] We underscore the unsettling continuities between militarism and displacement to foreground the systematic ways refugees are rendered as less than human subjects who are understood to be without history and agency at various levels of their containment and confinement in this country.

Unsettling conventional notions of refugee distress and need, we highlight how the refugee subject who has been apprehended in US and international law, essentialized in humanitarian discourse, and captured in cultural misrepresentations upend these discourses and critique their limitations. We build on these critiques by focusing on the imaginative ways that refugees re-create in their stories the formative ideas of community and collective justice. With the stories they tell and retell, refugees instruct us on what it means to be human and humane in the best and worst of times. Accordingly, *Departures* explores powerful forms of refugee critique, refusal, and community that challenge the notion of borders and legislation that police refugee migration and movement on a global scale. It traces the histories of militarism that intersect with race and racism in the United States and that drive the engine of war and imperialism outside it. This book puts pressure on the crucial point that empire building and war making at home works in parallel with empire building and war making abroad. Such logic also makes sense in the inverse; that is, we are *made* refugees and stateless by militaristic and racist enterprises, unsettling us throughout time and space even when we have settled in the United States.

For critical refugee studies (CRS) scholars (many of us are refugees for whom war is not merely a metaphor), this historic moment illustrates the ongoing-ness of hubris and militarism that underpin the making and unmaking of US empire. Hitting closer to home, the politics surrounding COVID-19 clarify the breadth of misery that touches many of the communities we care about, laying bare the razor-edged precarity of their lives. COVID-19 forces us to reflect on what it means to "stay at home" for not only refugees and the undocumented but also for those without homes (the unhoused) and for those whose homes are temporary and transient (refugee camp dwellers) or intolerable (victims of sexual and domestic abuse) and toxic (LGBTQ family members in homophobic households). In light of these untold tragedies, we stress the importance of bearing witness and grieving for those deemed "ungrievable" by the very powerful.[26] We side with Tahrir Hamdi when she conceptualizes memory as resistance: memory—in the face of empire—must remain "an active process of struggle which entails remembrance, interrogation, reclamation and resistance."[27] In recognition of Hamdi's words, we write this book in the active spirit of "remembrance" of our communities—to relay the stories of refugees and their struggles for voice, justice, and solidarity. Their stories serve as counternarratives against prevailing state and other imposed discourses. True to its genre of introductory books, *Departures* lays out in readable form a mode for critique and interrogation, reclamation and resistance.

This book's tone is rightly interlaced with both rage and optimism as a result of the phenomena we have been made to witness. As critical refugee studies scholars, we collaborate on this book and other CRS projects because we are enraged by the aggressions and hostilities that have been directed toward the globally displaced. At the same time, we are encouraged by BLM's civil unrest and disobedience that has taken hold of this country, a country whose "exceptionalism" has always been built on the backs of the enslaved, the oppressed, and the dispossessed. Participating in the protests as protesters ourselves, our energies have been reignited, as we and many others have endeavored to be at the forefront of rebellion against systemic racism.

About Collectivity

We take a moment here to put into focus the critical, collective energies that drive this book. Emphasizing collectivity and community, we reject the neoliberal ideology that dictates that the individual in society is an island of self-reliance. As we rely on each other in the worst of times, the community that we strive to form recognizes that mutual aid and support is necessary in our political climates both past and present. The Critical Refugee Studies

Collective (CRSC) is founded on this ethos; that is, together, we advocate for and "envision a world where all refugees are treated and embraced as fellow human beings with all fundamental rights and privileges."[28] We advance that *refugee* rights, defined as having access to appropriate shelter and food and being able to lead a life of dignity, are *human* rights. Along with this, we posit that refugees carry with them the power of their imaginations as they settle and resettle in lands not their own. *Departures* operates as an aperture into the refugee's world and the creative and critical potentiality that such a world offers. One of our key methodologies is to think and act collaboratively, a theory and practice we delve into throughout the book.

The writing of this book not only reflects our Collective's stance on refugees and human rights; it is also a collective effort itself. Exemplifying Helen Cafferty and Jeanette Clausen's argument that "collaboration, whatever the subject, whatever the agenda, becomes a political act with political consequences,"[29] our collaborations constitute acts of the political that counter the neoliberal impulse of the academy, which often privileges the work of the single author and the monograph, particularly in the Humanities. In the writing of this book, Yến Lê Espiritu, Lan Duong, Ma Vang, and Victor Bascara were the primary authors, but all CRSC members contributed their ideas and writing. In fact, it is this spirit of collaboration and support that had fashioned us from the beginning when we became a research group at the University of California Humanities Research Institute (UCHRI) in 2015. With a generous four-year grant from the University of California Office of the President (UCOP) in 2016, we continued to build the emerging field that is critical refugee studies. The Collective's activities in grant giving, teaching, and conducting research are explored further in the book's chapters and can be found on our website: criticalrefugeestudies.com.

If there has been joy in co-creating the communities we never would have thought possible, there has also been grief in witnessing the tumultuous events that have marked these years. We grieve for what has been lost during the pandemic, the lives lost due to state violence, and the trauma that has been wrought as a result of decades of deportations and violence at the US-Mexico border. In the end, however, we take heart in Arundhati Roy's words that the pandemic must, in the end, serve as a "portal, a gateway between one world to the next."[30] She writes that our choice is clear: "We can choose to walk through it, dragging the carcasses of our prejudice and hatred, our avarice, our data banks and dead ideas, our dead rivers and smoky skies behind us. Or we can walk through lightly, with little luggage, ready to imagine another world. And ready to fight for it."[31] Journeying through this portal and making our way to its end, we must be "ready to fight" and begin to imagine other possibilities and put into being another way of living. This book's trajectory insists on this momentum. At the same time that it details the injustices that have curtailed the lives of refugees, this work continually looks toward a more just future for our communities and points to the profundity of ideas and creativity that refugee stories carry. It is here that we will always begin.

Introduction

Departures

Committed to community-engaged scholarship, the Critical Refugee Studies Collective (CRSC) charts and builds the field of Critical Refugee Studies by centering refugee lives—and the creative and critical potentiality that such lives offer.

CRITICAL REFUGEE STUDIES COLLECTIVE, "Who We Are"

The objective of this book is to produce knowledge that is not only about but also by and for refugees. At its heart, critical refugee studies (CRS) is about *departures*: both the act of leaving and a divergence from a usual course of action. Grounded in refugee experiences of leave-taking, CRS emerges from a growing recognition of the need for a new approach to the study of refugees, a new *analytic* committed to realizing the meaningful change that refugee knowledges uniquely make desirable and achievable. Such outcomes might fit Audre Lorde's oft-cited notion of "genuine change" that eschews "the master's tools."[1] The conditions of emergence for CRS are akin to other emergent fields that arose in conjunction with movements seeking to address the problems and limitations of existing fields and methods. For these movements, existing fields and methods were coming to be seen as complicit with—or at least inadequate to confront—such conditions as systemic racism, patriarchy, settler/colonialism, militarism, capitalist exploitation, homophobia, transphobia, xenophobia, and environmental destruction. That complicity and inadequacy stem from deep-seated investments in conserving the supremacy of the modern (usually Western/colonized) world, including modernity's capacity to save the rest of the world from themselves and even ironically from modernity's own excesses.

Diverse and widespread movements for liberation have forged alternative approaches for imagining and realizing new possibilities. Challenging traditional paradigms that render difference knowable, manageable, and profitable, new fields—postcolonial studies, Indigenous studies, ethnic studies, gender studies, LGBTQIA+ studies, among others—have emerged to challenge the status quo and recognize what and who have been overlooked and underestimated, at times with genocidal consequences. Alongside this critical and creative turn, a growing body of knowledge production departs from existing ways refugees have been studied, insisting that the introduction to refugee worlds be rendered on refugees' own terms. The word *refugee* emerges in this work as a crucial analytical term and category for situating and naming a critique, as such terms as Black, Indigenous, Transgender, and many other (self-)identifying labels do, in necessary critical engagement with systemic structures and historically sedimented practices that reproduce the conscious and unconscious biases and inequalities of the status quo.

Departures: An Introduction to Critical Refugee Studies supports, contextualizes, and advances the field of CRS by providing a capacious account of its genealogy, methods, and key concepts, as well as its premises, priorities, and possibilities. It aims to be a resource and guide for all readers invested in addressing the concerns, perspectives, knowledge production, and global imaginings of refugees. For those who are unfamiliar with CRS, the book outlines the field's main tenets, questions, and concerns; and for scholars already engaged in the field, it offers new approaches that integrate theoretical rigor and policy concerns with refugees' rich and complicated lived worlds. For practitioners, *Departures* offers examples of how to link communities, movements, networks, artists, and academic institutions and to forge new and humane reciprocal paradigms, dialogues, visuals, and technologies that replace and reverse the dehumanization of refugees within imperialist gazes and frames, sensational stories, savior narratives, big data, colorful mapping, and spectator scholarship.

What must give way for the emergence of CRS? To answer, it would be instructive to consider the contexts and implications for invoking the term "refugee." As the Palestinian American scholar Edward W. Said has noted, "Refugees . . . are a creation of the twentieth-century state. The word 'refugee' has become a political one, suggesting large herds of innocent and bewildered people requiring urgent international assistance, whereas 'exile' carries with it, I think, a touch of solitude and spirituality."[2] "Refugee" is a term that does indeed suggest—nay, demand—"urgent international assistance." It then functions as a potent instrument of politics and culture, wielded by those in power in the exercise and legitimation of that power. In such usage, "refugee" operates as a mechanism of control and incorporation, inextricably linked to the necessary relief that is or is not provided by those with the resources and the will to provide, or withhold, that relief. CRS recognizes this condition, historically and in the present, and resists what that control and incorporation mean and produce.

The chapters that follow survey a range of institutions and disciplines that have been tasked with representing refugees, from the law and humanitarian organizations to cultural representations and the educational apparatus to militarism and migration enforcement. By focusing first on law, then on humanitarianism, and then on cultural representations, this book examines strategically how each of these key fields has made refugees into the objects of their disciplinary gazes. In coming to terms with each of these processes of objectification, it illuminates the ways in which refugee agency and epistemologies both draw on and exceed each of these three disciplines. As a field, CRS draws out the limitations, errors, and exclusions of these approaches, and it does so fundamentally rooted in refugee experience and the diverse and complex ways in which that experience uniquely manifests. As such, CRS is a dialectical combination of a critique of extant methods for knowing the refugee and a committed centering of refugee experiences *on refugees' own terms*, leading to a synthesis with grounded and far-reaching implications for change. "Refugee" can thus cease to be an instrument of incorporation and control and of the legitimation of the way things already are and become a means for grasping the lived historical experience of refugees and the compelling desires—political or otherwise—rooted in those experiences.

Departures is designed to bring both clarity and visibility to what has been uncertain and unseen, and complexity and de-emphasis to what has been oversimplified and hypervisible. Uncertainty and invisibility and oversimplification and hypervisibility have dogged refugees, given the radical diversity of refugees and the one-size-fits-all approaches that they have consistently faced. To return again to the words of Said, quoted above, the modern state created and duly politicized the refugee as such, "suggesting large herds of innocent and bewildered people requiring urgent international assistance." The worlds of refugees are much more, and much else, than this politicized bewilderment, innocence, and urgency conjured by the modern state, urgency that ironically can be undermined by the reifying use of statistics and maps and other management metrics by states and their agents. CRS is a way to seize control of image and narrative, by and for refugees, centered in refugee epistemologies and experiences, in ways that enable transformative interventions into legal and political arenas to engage with state structures but not be bound by them. This introductory book contributes to this ongoing project, keenly and necessarily aware of the metrics and definitions that are wielded and disseminated by highly empowered institutions and their agents.

In this volume, the rage, optimism, and "ungratefulness" (chapter 3) of refugees emerge as starting points for new and needed analytics that engage in "epistemic disobedience" of the colonial and unilateral knowledge production about refugees.[3] To grasp refugee agency and epistemology, we need to move beyond the official conceptions of urgency, innocence, and bewilderment, along with the "well-founded fear of persecution" (chapter 2), and resolutely toward formations of refugee livability, dignity, and criticality. As an example, refugee ingratitude and what you will read about as "refugee refusal" are points of access to distinctly discernible refugee agency and epistemology that break with the historically appointed role of refugees as seen entirely through a lens of precarity and gratitude. As discussed in chapter 3, in the familiar narrative of "crisis-rescue-gratitude," refugees have been gifted one capacity: to thank. Soft power, in the guise of humanitarianism, insidiously weaponizes gratitude (for the credited savior) such that any deviation from the unwavering demands placed on those surviving near-genocide and dispossession can only register as unintelligibility and/or vilification—as the ingratitude, backwardness, and ignorance of the pitiably traumatized. In this context, "refugee refusal" constitutes a process far more fraught and complex than can be explained as sellout opportunism, or doleful moral suasion, or conscientious disengagement. In any of these flowchart vectors, rational-choice calculation would be projected onto refugees, not in an effort to understand refugees, but more fundamentally to reaffirm the supremacy of the righteous savior to govern, whose selfhood needs alterity in the form of being thanked. This book recognizes those conditions as structural and historical, as a baseline for critical approaches to become not only possible, but necessary for the decolonial project that refugees manifest. Those refugee manifestations are decolonial insofar as they are evidence of that which political and cultural representation has failed. And these manifestations of "epistemic disobedience" can emerge in diverse forms, such as in narrated experiences collected and disseminated by scholarly investigators and in creative production in the cultural sphere, discursive and otherwise.

To introduce readers to CRS, the central interventions of this book are as follows:

- The identification and critique of key disciplines and institutions that have represented refugees, especially via the law and state apparatuses (mainly in chapters 1 and 2), humanitarianism (mainly in chapter 3), and diverse forms of refugee cultural production (mainly in chapter 4).
- The identification and critique of key ideologies that have dictated and limited what refugees can mean (all four chapters).

- The recognition and appreciation of refugee epistemologies, creativity, and life-sustaining practices (all four chapters).

Together, these interventions recognize refugee life-making in its complexity while pushing against conventions in anthropology, sociology, political science, human rights discourse, and the legal apparatus. Throughout this book, refugee complexity is evident both through (re)examining existing representations and through appreciating refugee-generated articulations.

While the book's chapters ostensibly and strategically focus on law, humanitarianism, and culture, their interventions are interwoven throughout to generate a collective analytic that both consistently confronts existing approaches to refugees and demonstrates intersectional interventions that become possible when centering and prioritizing refugee experiences and epistemologies. This centering and prioritizing of refugees is crucial for ensuring that refugees are not treated as a passive and transparent source for content or data for social sciences or for unreconstructed sentimentalism in the cultural sphere.

Critical Refugee Studies as Such

Departures synthesizes and distills the substantial, resonant, and growing scholarly *and* creative work that has begun to cohere as critical refugee studies. Its goal is to articulate the genealogies, methods, and objectives that build and support CRS in an explicit and strategic way. There are at least three related genres that this book may resonate with, though not quite fit exactly: the textbook, the reference book, and the policy brief. Like a textbook, this volume provides an analytical framework, pertinent information, and points of access for understanding a subject. But the interdisciplinarity of CRS and the diversity of forms it can take resist containment by extant fields. Like a reference book, this volume is a collection of key concepts and historical events and policy manifestations pertinent to CRS. But it is also not explicitly set up along the lines of a unified chronology like a timeline, of conceptual fixity like a dictionary, or of institutional legitimation like a policy analysis. Finally, like a policy brief, this book invokes the formation of pertinent policy and its implementation and has the potential to shape policy because of that. However, unlike a policy brief, these propositions not only address possibilities within established parameters but also call into question those very parameters in order to shift the paradigm toward alternative approaches and epistemologies.

This commitment to bringing about change resonates with existing movements, including their methods and objectives, even if the specificities of refugees may strain the unity and coherence of this new field. So another key function of this volume, especially given its critical dimensions, is to serve as a *re-introduction*, as a way of helping to identify resonant and connected critical approaches that can appreciate the interventions of refugee subjectivity for other fields and methods, movements and communities—a strategic tool for finding a contingent common ground while respecting meaningful differences that cannot and should not be elided. Perhaps an illustrative parallel for such critical and advocacy work would be how the Black Lives Matter movement—invoked in the prologue—has needed to address the premises and implications of those who counter with "all lives matter." The claim that "all lives matter" has historically served to devalue Black lives by materially and ideologically upholding white supremacy, insidiously expressed as "all lives," in contradiction to racist slavery, genocide, colonialism, and persistent inequality in myriad forms. Or in another related context, "all lives matter" is an approach similar to how the shrewd organizers of Proposition 209 a quarter century ago deviously and deceptively called it the "California Civil Rights Initiative," when in actuality its dismantling of social justice legislation is exactly the opposite of protecting civil rights for the historically and persistently discriminated against. CRS, then, in no small part, is focused on addressing misperceptions, particularly the tokenism and photo-ops that refugees have been subjected to by the powers that be who trot out rescued refugees as evidence of the legitimacy of the world they made and are perpetuating (chapter 4).

Given that *refugee* is a vernacular word in wide circulation as well as a specialized term in highly regulated institutional spaces, *Departures* can be thought of as a primer that can help with the navigation between diverse, intersecting, and divergent conceptions and usages. There are instances when *refugee* is implied or projected onto a situation or person or group while not actually being invoked explicitly, including by the migrant subjects themselves. And there are other instances when *refugee* is actively and conspicuously claimed or eschewed by the state and its political, cultural, and economic institutions.[4] Accordingly, CRS intervenes in existing and historical uses of the term "refugee," and much of the first part of this book is rightly devoted to that. Although "refugee" is a term that can, and frequently does, evoke emotional responses, such as sorrow, pity, entitlement, fear, outrage, shame, righteous indignation, and schadenfreude, and much more, CRS demands that we center "refugee" experience, especially that which is in excess of the methods and modes and spaces of meaning and representation in and through which refugees have systematically been cast: historical events (especially war and environmental conditions), discriminatory policy and legislation, nonsecular persecutions, and other conditions that necessitate flight.

We stand at a crucial moment of refugee uprising and innovation in the face of persistent and renewed perils. A potential resistance to this work comes not just from the xenophobic, cruel, and stingy but also from those who seek validation from assisting those in need, mainly in the form of refugee gratitude and perhaps also refugee forgiveness for "errors" of the past, such as dispossession, conquest, slavery, genocide, exclusion. Being forcibly incorporated into an economy of gratitude has been a defining condition of refugees, a world order for making others look good, or at least less bad (see chapter 3). Such motivations have real consequences; the effective abandonment of concerns is not the answer, as current US practices since at least early 2017 have made widespread. A case in point: the 2017–21 US administration, with its tightening restrictions on the capaciousness of the category "refugee" and with particular viciousness in the recent family-splitting treatment of refugees from Central America fleeing violence, systemic poverty, and persecution and the well-founded fear of it.[5] These critical analyses of the US state are worthwhile, but they are effectively assessments that center hegemonic institutions—impactful as they clearly are—that are not the sole focus or motivating priority of CRS. Departing from the hegemonic objectification and dehumanization of refugees, CRS is committed to a critical analysis that emerges from the worlds and epistemologies of refugees. This shifted focus does not replace existing, institution-focused approaches, and it is also not invested in the preservation or undermining of institutions. If preserving or undermining happens, that is a collateral effect to the more central priority: *allowing the worlds of refugees to be evident, on their own terms, as much as possible.*

We view CRS as an expression and instrument of a movement of diverse constituencies. The particular formation of CRS that led to this volume sprang from a growing network of engaged and interdisciplinary scholars, especially the authors of this volume who initially convened at the University of California Humanities Research Institute (UCHRI) in Irvine in 2015. Through expanded efforts, in part supported by a University of California Office of the President grant (2016–2020), this collective grew to integrate a broader convergence of not only scholars but also artists and community organizers and K–12 students and teachers. A great many of these individuals have direct connections to refugee experiences and communities, and that network represents both traditional and especially emergent disciplines, in formal training as well as in current faculty positions, all committed to examining how the putative urgencies of refugees ironically displace actual refugee agency and epistemologies when empowered institutions exercise their power to manage and represent refugees. It is not a coincidence that this critical work converges with and productively grows out of critical race studies, ethnic studies, Indigenous studies, postcolonial and decolonial studies, gender studies, LGBTQIA+ studies, migration studies, environmental studies, food studies, and area studies, as well as sociology, political science, history, law, religion, philosophy, english, music, dance, comparative literature, film/media, anthropology, and more.

Since 2016, through the efforts of the Critical Refugee Studies Collective, manifestations of CRS work have been diverse. They include numerous community events, multiple academic conferences, a book series in partnership with the University of California Press, an innovative and interactive website (criticalrefugeestudies. com), a flowering of podcasts, a K–12 teaching institute, university courses across the curriculum, a grants program, art exhibitions, documentaries, ethnographies, dance performances, and more. We hope that this book, which recognizes and identifies the emergence of CRS as a broad-based movement that is both critical and creative, helps and encourages new work that will advance what we express in this volume. Indeed, *Departures* is a way to distill some of the main insights, effective methods, and pertinent materials of this expanding and expansive body of work. We encourage you to consult criticalrefugeestudies.com for more information and material, including details about scores of projects through the grants program, the multimedia story maps, the blog and creative entries from scholars, organizers, and artists, an ever-expanding keywords glossary, and links to further resources.

CRS Methodologies: Re-storying, Feminist Refugee Epistemology, Collaboration

Departing from the asymmetrical representational apparatus that renders refugees hypervisible and invisible, erasing their humanity, heterogeneity, and agency, critical refugee studies introduces new methods to (re)situate refugee epistemologies and lifeworlds at the very center of knowledge production. *Storytelling*—or *re-storying*, to use the Nigerian writer Chinua Achebe's term—is particularly important for forging a different and needed analytic on refugees. Achebe, who envisions "postcolonial cultures taking shape story by story," coins the term "re-storying" to name the process of "tak[ing] back the narrative" of "peoples who had been knocked silent by all kinds of dispossession," in the hope that the re-storying will result in a "balance of stories among the world's peoples."[6] Building on Achebe's concept, Khatharya Um, who painstakingly collected and curated over 250 Cambodian survivor narratives, defines re-storying as the process of conceptualizing survivor-refugees as "experiencing subjects": "It is to rewrite the individual, the human, back where necropolitics had sought to vacate, and to ground a macro discussion of political forces and global machinations in the micro details and nuances of real lives," thereby balancing the power to describe, to narrate, and to legitimate.[7] In re-storying dominant narratives and visualizations, CRS infuses refugee stories—big and small, disturbing and touching, violent and loving—with an insurgent energy and purpose, insisting that these stories "are worthy of the power and dignity of literature,"[8] as well as films, paintings, foodways, archives, websites, and more.

In interpreting refugee modes of re-storying, we deepen the study of refugees by focusing on the narratives and images that refugees use to tell their stories. Against the public erasure of such complex stories, we offer a feminist approach in examining the intersections between private grief and public commemoration, the listening for unsaid things by relying on other senses such as feelings and emotions, and the looking for the hidden political forces within the site of intimate domestic and familial interaction. We call this mode of analysis Feminist Refugee Epistemology (FRE), and we define the tenets of FRE as a CRS methodology throughout the book. At its essence, FRE resists the objectification of refugees and their bodies and eschews representations of refugees in terms of the spectacular, the iconic, and the figural. Instead, FRE insists on a kind of looking practice that interrogates the less visible and more quotidian details of refugee lives. By positing a Feminist Refugee Epistemology, CRS takes seriously the hidden and overt injuries that refugees experience but also the joy and survival practices that play out in the domain of the everyday; and to mark the broken trajectories but also the moments of action—indeed, of creation—as refugees search for and insist on their right to more. In this methodology the subjectivities and stories of refugees breathe and come alive for us.

Interlinked with re-storying and FRE is collaboration, a profoundly rich method that allows us to imagine other possibilities through collective thought and action. Collaborative practice lies at the center of our group's intellectual and political mode of being, as it expresses the "multi-voiced, multilayered process that becomes intrinsic" to how we write, reflect, and revolt together.[9] Indeed, our formation as a collective is premised on a kind of critical collaboration that operates as both strategy and method, the results of which have yielded formative imaginings and conversations within and beyond academia. In this, we draw from the deep well of power that comes from collaborative acts, which upend the individualistic and neoliberal ethos that often undergirds dominant notions of creativity and criticality. For to be (em)powered by a sense of community is to think expansively about survival and sustenance in the long term. And to act collaboratively for this same community is to learn by heart what Audre Lorde reminded us of long ago—that "without community, there is no liberation, no future."[10] Accordingly, in the book's conclusion, we invite our communities to enact together our collective liberation.

Book Organization and Arc

What follows are ways of rethinking refugees along three main themes: law/politics, humanitarianism, and media/culture. The prologue, which situates this book in the cascading crises and social movements of the present, first brings you deeper into the interventions and implications of CRS, particularly the importance of connections that refugee critique has with critiques of imperialism, racism, patriarchy, and militarism. A key site of convergence between these critiques and refugee critique is Enlightenment liberalism and contemporary neoliberalism. That is, ideas and ideals of rights, of the human, of equality, of freedom, of sovereignty are in the abstract laudable, but in practice they have consistently been materially realized through the rightlessness, subhumanity, inequality, bondage, and dispossession of great masses. Indeed, the introduction to refugee worlds opens out to multiple histories and experiences of colonialism, militarism, racism, and displacement. Although this book mentions other imperial regimes that are implicated in creating the conditions of forced migration, its critique of empire is mainly directed at US empire.

Chapters 1 and 2, as tandem chapters, focus on law, politics, and policy. This is the strategic point of departure as these areas are where the concept of the refugee has tended to demand the most rigid and sustained fixity. State power as persecution and the withholding or failure of state protection from persecution have traditionally been where refugees are in effect created. While the power of the law is vast, refugee critique shows that the law is not a totalizing force in refugees' lives. These chapters critically juxtapose policy analysis and historical narrative with refugees' poetic expression to track the formative role of the law, the law's ongoing limitations, and ways in which refugees engage, critique, and evade the law and in doing so assert and exercise agency that the law cannot fully account for and manage. In other words, refugee agency demonstrates the capacities and limits of state power, in the hands of those who have ostensibly been utterly formed by it, both as victim and saved, as exile and asylee. Refugee agency beyond legal categories includes but then well exceeds the dictates of compliance and transgression. Phenomena like internal displacement, occupation, gender and sexual persecution, and myriad forms of dispossession that do not conform to existing statutory bases of discrimination create category crises for refugee law and policy, with potentially dire consequences for those who are misread and/or are unseen by that law. Such misreading and invisibility can enhance vulnerability, persecution, exploitation, and denial of protections. A refugee critique of the law, one rooted in refugee-centered epistemologies, makes these limitations evident and is a necessary step toward addressing what can be literally fatal flaws with extant legal instruments.

Where a capacity for extralegal agency can become particularly evident is through culture, from arts and media to culture in an anthropological sense. Chapter 3 uses a mix of cultural texts to identify what is a necessary but potentially uncomfortable site of critical refugee agency: ingratitude. This chapter sheds light on the deceptively complex and ideologically fraught dynamic between the vulnerable dispossessed and the humanitarian aid givers, in the various forms that that takes. Gratitude is a viable and understandable reaction to having been rescued from annihilation. In that economy, this chapter asks, what does the rescuer get from this transaction? One outcome is a profound affirmation of the rightness of their worldview, that their civilization and the power it has long wielded over others are legitimate and benevolent, what Aihwa Ong has called "compassionate domination."[11] This affirmation can be an especially desirable outcome for rescuers in the face of widespread and often violent resistance to the imperial idea. Noting the complicatedness of exhibiting (un)gratefulness for refugees, this chapter engages the concept "refugee refusal," showing how it can be subtle, complex, and radically difficult to reconcile with current paradigms of interpretation. This strategy of ingratitude emerges in literary texts but also amid the dramatically uneven power dynamic of earnest teachers and their refugee students in underresourced communities. In addition to the illustrative culture texts, chapter 3 draws on testimonials given during a critical refugee studies K–12 teaching symposium in San Diego featuring dialogues between teachers, students, and parents, and, importantly, using translators. This community dialogue allowed the students and parents to assert a more expansive notion of "intelligence," one that is unmoored from the likely unconscious association of intelligence and English proficiency, a connection that has been overwhelming for these students and their families, many of whom are already multilingual (e.g., French and Kirundi) but who are still learning English and therefore have been made to feel less intelligent than they know themselves to be. In an educational setting, "refugee refusal" is too easily dismissed as deficiency and codified as academic failure. CRS recognizes that such failures are the academy's and not the refugees'. This kind of pushback is not new, as generations of educational reform movements can readily attest. The need for such pushback by refugees connects CRS to those other movements (e.g., labor studies, ethnic studies, queer studies) while also recognizing the persistence of hegemonic tendencies in the education apparatus, despite the important transformative work of those movements.

Chapter 4 is especially attuned to the means through which refugee agency and epistemologies are communicated to diverse audiences. Arresting images of so-called trauma porn have consistently been the platform of visibility for refugees, creating a circumstance where anything else is either silent/unseen or unintelligible or terrifying. With particular attention not only to the analysis of cultural works but also to the infrastructures of creation, reception, distribution, and, at times, recovery, this chapter provides the reader with a method for appreciating "refugee creativity and criticality" in the curious dynamic of refugees being at once "invisible and hypervisible."

We end the book with an epilogue, in the form of a CRSC letter to the United Nations High Commissioner for Refugees (UNHCR) in anticipation of its seventy-fifth anniversary in December 2025. The second-person address, which follows the form of James Baldwin's "My Dungeon Shook: Letter to My Nephew on the One Hundredth Anniversary of the Emancipation,"[12] offers us a way to speak directly to the UNHCR (and the international community) to demand a rethinking of their definitions, approaches, and knowing of refugees. As we insist in the letter, *there has to be—and is—a better way.*

Coda: "all about that extra / inch"

CRS is committed to a nonhierarchical diversity of forms and platforms for doing meaningful work. So here, without further comment, is a work of poetry, supported by a CRSC grant, as a closing, stand-alone demonstration of CRS in action.[13]

the reason we indent

BOONMEE YANG

we're instructed
by white men to indent our paragraphs at half an inch
regardless of how our lives began but I see how
their history books have hundreds of pages of paragraphs

that can afford losing thousands of half inches' worth of words
leaving out their crimes of horror while my people
only have two paragraphs to fit in everything wrong about my
    culture
and you might think losing an inch
is no big deal yet white men are
all about that extra
inch

1   *A Refugee Critique of the Law*
On "Fear and Persecution"

*But in our camp, his story was everyone's story, a single tale of dispossession,
of being stripped to the bones of one's humanity, of being dumped like
rubbish into refugee camps unfit for rats.*

SUSAN ABULHAWA, *Mornings in Jenin*

*We talk of regional conflicts, of economic and social crises, of political
instability, of abuses of human rights, of racism, religious intolerance,
inequalities between rich and poor, hunger, over-population, under-
development and . . . I could go on and on. Each and every one of these
impediments to humanity's pursuit of well-being are also among the root
causes of refugee problems [sic].*

POUL HARTLING, UN High Commissioner for Refugees, 1978–1985

We are at a moment of renegotiating what it means to be a refugee.
While the definition of *refugee* stipulated by the 1951 Convention
Relating to the Status of Refugees (hereafter referred to as "the
Convention") remains the international standard for the granting
of refugee status,[1] it emerged as a legal mandate that was shaped
by the geopolitical exigencies of Europe and the historical conditions of World War II. The Convention has become increasingly

irrelevant to today's crises and to the conditions and characteristics of refugees they produce. Indeed, the complex conditions facing many dislocated communities in this age of militarization, globalization, and interdependence cannot easily be classified neatly as economic or political causes of migration. Thus they cannot be adjudicated on the bases of "fear and persecution" that were stipulated by the Convention. This chapter advances our critical refugee studies (CRS) critique of the refugee protection regime that is founded on and continues to be informed by the 1951 Convention that anchors protection in a *temporally* and *spatially* restricted concept of fear, specifically, in terms of which fear can/not be recognized and where "fearful" people can/not go.

In the face of massive post–World War II displacement, the 1951 Convention was formulated and passed to address the need for an international response to the "refugee problem" and to establish an international standard for the protection of the forcibly displaced.[2] Affirming the principles that "human beings shall enjoy fundamental rights and freedoms without discrimination" and that refugees should have "the widest possible exercise of these fundamental rights and freedoms,"[3] the Convention codified the language of protection according to the principle of *non-refoulement,* which stipulates that asylum seekers cannot be returned to conditions of duress.[4] A foundational refugee protection framework, the Convention definition of *refugee* remains a primary point of reference in the discourse of refugee law seven decades after its ratification.

Refugee situations that emerged in the decades following the ratification of the Convention have increasingly tested the integrity and viability of its framework in the contemporary context, as well as the fundamental assumptions on which it rests. While the UN considers repatriation one of the "durable solutions" to mass displacement, it does not, for instance, take into consideration the fact that for communities such as the Palestinians whose homeland has been erased by settler colonialism and militarized occupation (see chapter 2) and Pacific Islanders who have been displaced by rising seawater, *return* is fraught or impossible, though it may be desired and hoped for. Rather than resettlement or repatriation, protracted unsettlement or "warehousing" has become an increasingly common feature of the global refugee experience.

Our critique exposes how the contextual particularities of the Convention's genesis accounts for its inherent limitations. We argue that the Convention framework, on which many ensuing refugee laws and protocols are based, makes no room for the multiplicity and complexity of refugee claims and as such is as important for what it excludes as what it includes. This chapter interrogates and problematizes the concept of fear, especially as it dehistoricizes ongoing violence and discounts and erases the *longue durée* of the conditions that engender many instances of global dislocations. It also critiques the tethering of refugee status not only to the demonstration of fear, but, simultaneously and of ultimate importance, to the geopolitical and spatial contingent of border crossing.

The Limits of Refugee Law

Its stated commitment to refugee protection notwithstanding, the 1951 Convention contains very narrow parameters that limit its wider applicability. While protection is a central pillar, the provisions of the Convention applied only to persons who were forcibly displaced before January 1, 1951, and those already considered refugees under the 1926 and 1928 Arrangements and the 1933 and 1938 Conventions. Though the language of the Convention did include the clause "Europe and elsewhere," the populations that had to be resettled and reintegrated in the immediate postwar years were essentially European, many with shared linguistic and cultural traditions and socioeconomic backgrounds. The Convention, as such, pertained essentially to Europe and was Europe-centric in its formulation.

The Convention, moreover, limits the types of persecution that can be considered in adjudicating fear. In addition to those already recognized as refugees under previous arrangements, Article I of the 1951 Convention defines a refugee as any person who

> as a result of events occurring before 1 January 1951 and owing to well-founded fear of being persecuted for reasons of race, religion, nationality, membership of a particular social group or political opinion, is outside the country of his nationality and is unable or, owing to such fear, is unwilling to avail himself of the protection of that country; or who, not having a nationality and being outside the country of his former habitual residence as a result of such events, is unable or, owing to such fear, is unwilling to return to it.[5]

While it identifies race, religion, nationality, membership in a particular social group, and political opinion as the recognized bases of persecution, it does not include generalized violence. Nor does it address other catalysts of mass migration besides persecution and human rights violations. Environmental degradation and injustice, famine, and calamities such as rising sea levels, floods, and droughts have displaced people from their homes and communities and engendered mass migration, in some instances without the possibility of return. For those dislocated by these conditions, migration is not a planned "voluntary" option. The question of constrained volition aside, the fixed binary of politically engendered and economically motivated displacement does not account for the ways in which economic conditions can be and have been politicized. Under the Khmer Rouge, for instance, food was deliberately wielded as an implement of the genocidal state to subjugate or punish, resulting in the deaths of hundreds of thousands of Cambodians.[6]

The reductionist approach to forced migration, furthermore, fails to consider the intersecting, overlapping, and compounding factors that compel migration.[7] Mutually reinforcing links between structural inequities and ethnic, racial, political, and religious persecution, or between factors such as environmental degradation, ethnic conflict, patriarchy, and gendered violence, further challenge the fixed and false binary of political and economic motivators of migration. As the UNHCR has noted, "Refugees, stateless people, and the internally displaced . . . often reside in climate change 'hotspots' and may be exposed to secondary displacement."[8] Though this statement is a nod of recognition to the increasing complexity of refugee experiences, it only registers concerns for climate change impact *as it relates to* refugees or already displaced communities, and only as a "secondary" cause of displacement. It does not, however, address climate-related disasters as catalysts of mass displacement in and of themselves, including cross-border movement, often into inhospitable contexts. Neither does it address the fact that these conditions can be of such magnitude and severity—tantamount to "generalized violence"—as to preclude return. Similarly, while the 2018 Global Compact on Refugees acknowledges that "climate, environmental degradation and natural disasters increasingly interact with the drivers of refugee movements,"[9] it merely recognizes such interactivity while explicitly discounting climate disasters as direct causes of refugee movements.[10] At present, the term "climate refugee" does not exist in international law.

As a result of proliferating climate-related disasters in many parts of the world and in the absence of an internationally binding protection provision, "environmentally displaced persons" (EDPs), a term that UN agencies prefer over "climate refugees," have increasingly comprised a large proportion of the internally displaced. As with nonrecognized politically dislocated communities, the label "displaced" assigned to climate refugees implies a certain temporariness of the situation that belies, as in the case of sinking islands, the protracted or permanent nature of their displacement.

The plight of climate refugees also exposes the intersecting and compounding factors, including different forms and layers of state violence, that inform not only how the experiences of forced migration are to be differently understood but also how the complex and overlapping claims can and should be redressed, and by whom. As Shweta Jayawardhan argues, socioeconomic inequality and marginalization of vulnerable communities through discriminatory zoning practices and protection decisions based on property value account for the disparity in who is displaced by the effects of climate change.[11]

Furthermore, the existing refugee law does not account for instances in which the decision to flee is compelled, not by a specific fear, but by systemic oppression and the daily assault on people's lives, including as a result of their Indigeneity, race/ethnicity, sexual identities, religion, or political affiliation, that have become overbearing and unbearable. Even within its restrictive parameters, the 1951 Convention and subsequent 1967 Protocol never defined the notion of persecution, though it is the bedrock of the protective mandate. In the same vein, there is no definition or consensual understanding of what constitutes "a particular social group," which is one of the stated categories of persecution, or whether classes of persons such as women and "homosexuals" not included in the 1951 Convention but who nonetheless face persecution can be subsumed under that category. It was not until 2002 that the UN issued additional guidelines for determining gender-related persecution and "membership of a particular social group."[12] While noting that "women" are considered a social category with "innate and immutable characteristics . . . who are frequently treated differently than men,"[13] the guidelines stipulate that membership in a social group alone is insufficient for making a refugee status claim, which must be established on the basis of a well-founded fear of being persecuted because of such membership.[14] This requirement by the law to prove specific risks due to one's membership in an "innate" social category fixes gender as a singular issue that does not intersect with one's race, sex, class, or social and political values. The presumption of the mutually exclusive nature of these categories is contested by the UNHCR Asylum Lawyers Project's interpretation of gender-based claims, which argues that "women who transgress social mores may also be viewed in some societies as having made a religious or political statement. Thus, persecution in such settings might effectively be linked to religion or political opinion, actual or imputed, as well as membership in a particular social group."[15]

The definitional and categorical constraints embedded in the laws are particularly evident in the case of queer refugees. In determining fear, Turkey, one of the largest refugee receiving countries, for example, adheres to the Convention definition of gender and sexuality as inherent characteristics and not social categories. Refugee law's heteronormative paradigm reinforces the nation-state's liberal humanitarian project such that asylum claims can only emerge as individualized testimonies of migrant exceptionalism, state benevolence, and "citizenship-for-all."[16] Speaking of the need of queer asylum seekers to prove their deservingness to the Turkish state, Mert Koçak notes that this group has been "asked to turn their complicated experiences of political, social and economic displacement into coherent stories of 'well-founded fear' of strictly political persecution as a result of their sexuality and gender identities."[17] The multiplicity of issues that affect queer refugees' lives that are not inherent to gender and/or sexual identification must be muted to demonstrate deservingness. To prove deservingness within the state's liberal humanitarian paradigm and claim a right to stay requires visibility as the "good (queer) refugee." This image is often mobilized against the undeserving refugee and asylum seeker who is deemed undocumented, heterosexual, reproductively threatening, poor, and criminal.[18] Hence, heteronormative queerness, what Jasbir Puar calls homonationalism, not only defines deservingness of asylum, but also the asylee's contributions to racial capitalist productivity, national reproductivity, and the nation-state's narrative of "sexual and racial emancipation."[19]

The Internally Displaced

Further delimiting its applicability, the Convention anchors refugee status not only on a narrow definition of fear but also on the precondition of cross-border flight by stipulating that a refugee must be "outside the country of his nationality." In doing so, it divests those fleeing the same conditions but unable to cross national borders who are now categorized as "internally displaced people" (IDP) of the claim to protection. There is, in fact, no single international body that is entrusted with protection of and assistance to IDPs. By using cross-border movement as a measure of legitimate fear and an index of an individual's inability to obtain protection, the law hitches the fate of IDPs to the responsibility of the sovereign state that has proven, in repeated instances, to be not the protector but the transgressor of their rights.

As of 2019, IDPs worldwide, including those displaced by armed conflict, generalized violence, persecution of different forms, development projects, and climate disasters, number some 45.7 million people who, by virtue of being unwilling or unable to cross national borders, are now outside the Convention's protective mantle.[20] In the absence of a robust accountability system, IDPs are difficult to track, itself an added dimension of vulnerability, though incontestably they constitute significant numbers. According to the United Nations Department of Economic and Social Affairs (UNDESA) (2016), the scale of internal displacement may be over three times that of cross-border migration. In Syria, in addition to the millions of war refugees who have crossed borders in search of refuge, over six million are internally displaced. In Ethiopia, whose forced migrants are among the largest and most recent, 98 percent are internally displaced.

Unable to count on either the protection of their own government or that of international agencies given their lack of special status in international law, IDPs are among the most vulnerable of the displaced populations. Many remain in close proximity to or are trapped in conflict zones and are vulnerable to many abuses, including the risk of being used as human shields. In addition, the overwhelming majority of IDPs are women and children. Already vulnerable to gender-based violence and discrimination, women caught in the crosshairs of conflict are especially at risk given the prevalence of sexual violence both as a systematically wielded tool of political persecution and as a feature of generalized violence in war. The difficulty of tracking IDPs also translates into the difficulty of ensuring accountability, which is particularly problematic in the case of those displaced by conflict but denied refugee status who are compelled to seek return by the untenability of their situation.

The State-Centered Framework

A key challenge of the existing international refugee protection regime that is founded on and continues to be informed by the 1951 Convention is the nation-state framework that aligns rights with citizenship and national borders. Embedded in this conceptualization of rights and obligations is the notion of the sovereign state as the protector of all individuals residing within its territorial domain. By extension, the assumption is that divestment of protection only occurs after forced migrants have crossed the borders, an assumption that is constantly unraveled by numerous instances of state-sponsored violence against its own people.

In this transnational moment when globalizing forces have destabilized the totalizing power of the state, the global refugee conditions and rising protectionism that have seen increased stringent border controls and anti-immigrant measures are somber reminders of the persisting reality of state power. Through policies, failed governance, or malevolent neglect, states not only catalyze the refugee condition in many instances but also determine possibilities of and impediments to its resolution. States hold the ultimate right to grant or deny refugee status, which paves the way for further politicization of what is purportedly a humanitarian consideration. All too often, simple denial of the existence of a refugee condition or mere substitution of the term "refugee" with "displaced person," a recourse adopted by Thailand in the face of refugee exodus from Cambodia, Laos, and Việt Nam in the late 1970s, allows states to do away with the responsibilities to protect refugees. State prerogatives and state-centered frameworks thus produce and perpetuate refugees and inform refugee discourse.

Equally significant and constraining is the notion of sovereignty and a sovereign state's sacrosanct right over its populace. In the context of the international refugee regime, this has translated into an inability or unwillingness of external powers and international organizations to address issues of the internally displaced even in the face of human rights violations. The issue of state sovereignty has stood and continues to stand in tension not only with the mandate of international protection but also with the international community's efforts to prevent a refugee condition from emerging in the first place.

State prerogatives extend to the right to endorse or not endorse any international understandings. Even with the widely adopted 1951 and 1967 Conventions, many refugee-receiving states are nonsignatories or may have ratified one agreement and not the other. Turkey, for instance, retains the geographic limitation of the 1951 UN Convention and as such recognizes only refugees from Europe, despite being host to the largest community of Syrians displaced by the ongoing conflict, totaling over 3.6 million.[21] Terms such as "protocol" and "declaration" are not legally binding and defer to states' decision and political will to abide by them, which undermines the consistency and assurance of protection. All these issues undercut the ability of the international community to protect and assist vulnerable populations, to effectively and consistently enforce the protective measures that do exist, albeit with grave limitations, or ensure states' compliance with international law.

Contested Temporality of the "Refugee Crisis"

In addition to the limiting parameters discussed above, the refugee regime that remains in place today rests on problematic assumptions. While refugee conditions are often spoken of in terms of "crisis," hence assumed to be temporary, approximately 78 percent of the world's refugee populations currently are considered to be in a "protracted refugee situation."[22] As of 2015, about 72 percent of those protracted situations have lasted for over twenty years.[23] Moreover, according to the UNHCR, not only has the number of protracted situations greatly increased, but refugees are spending longer periods in displacement, averaging ten years in general and twenty-one years among those in protracted conditions.[24] While the term "protracted" is useful for highlighting the enduring condition of displacement, it does not capture the dehumanization of this state of exception that is encoded in the term "warehousing" designated for such situations.

These conditions of precarity are largely obscured by the fact that over 80 percent of the world's forcibly displaced, including those officially recognized as refugees, remain in the Global South, with four out of five remaining in countries contiguous to their homeland from which they had fled.[25] In the late 1990s, Africa hosted more refugees than any other part of the world.[26] According to the UNHCR 2016 survey, Lebanon, Jordan, Turkey, and Chad were the countries that hosted the most refugees relative to their populations.[27]

The structure of refugee resettlement, as such, reflects a failure of the law, one that produces a different kind of refugee waiting, namely, in camps in first countries of refuge where they are subjected to inadequate protection of their human rights and other rights and to stringent refugee screenings for resettlement. In what Jennifer Hyndman terms "preventive protection," Western states' commitment to refugee law is transactional in the form of fiscal transfers to the UN and developing states to build camps where refugees would be contained in Global South countries rather than permitted to seek direct refuge in Western states.[28] In this "spatialized strategy of assisting displaced persons within countries at war rather than as refugees in countries nearby,"[29] as Hyndman puts it, what undergirds refugee policy is a "donor-sponsored effort to contain forced migration" rather than a humanitarian practice (see chapter 3).[30]

Amendments to the 1951 Convention

All this points to the need for a more capacious, more robust, and more consistently enforced international protection regime that would reflect newly emerging and widening refugee situations. From the time of its inception, the international community has recognized the limits of the 1951 Convention; in light of the gaps, the UN itself had called upon its High Commissioner to use their good office to extend care and assistance to those in need regardless of status. The appeal notwithstanding, with limited resources and political will and active objections from countries in the Global North, priorities are given to those with formal refugee designation, and those in need but outside of this category are at best peripheralized and at worse actively penalized. The limitations of the Convention were made acutely evident by resurgent refugee situations in the ensuing decades that necessitated the rethinking and expansion of the earlier provisions. Decolonization and post-independence conflicts engendered new and different refugee conditions, no longer confined to specific continents and catalyzed by forces and circumstances not addressed in the existing conventions.

These developments underscored the limits of the existing protective regime and the need for a more expansive protective framework. The Protocol Relating to the Status of Refugee that was ratified in 1967 freed the 1951 provisions of their temporal and geographic tethers, extending them to refugees globally. Efforts were also taken, largely at the regional states' level, to further amend the definition of *refugee*. The 1969 Convention Governing the Specific Aspects of Refugee Problems enacted by the Organization of African Unity (OAU) expanded the basis of fear to include "external aggression, occupation, foreign domination, or events seriously disturbing public order in either part or the whole of his country of origin or nationality."[31] Subsequently, the Cartagena Declaration on Refugees issued by Latin American states in 1984 formally included "persons fleeing generalized violence of armed conflict, internal aggression, and massive violation of human rights or other circumstances which have seriously disturbed public order."[32] Both measures were intended to fill the definitional gaps in the earlier understandings by recognizing generalized violence and "public disorder" as bases of fear and persecution and, in the case of the Cartagena Declaration, by extending the categories beyond external war and occupation to include "internal aggression and massive violation of human rights," crucial steps given the internal conflicts and massive human rights abuses perpetuated by right-wing dictatorships in the region at the time of the declaration. While both the 1969 and 1984 amendments recognize public disorder as a bona fide criterion, as in the case of the term "persecution," they defer to state and regional discretion to determine what constitutes "public disorder." Significantly, though other states can adopt this more expansive definition, both understandings were essentially aimed at regional states in Africa and Latin America, respectively.

The Politicization of Humanitarianism

By addressing human rights violation as a source of persecution, the Cartagena Declaration points to an important constraint in the implementation of international refugee law, which is the intrusion of Cold War politics in the adjudication of fear and persecution in the post–World War II context. Until the passage of the Refugee Act in 1980, Cold War politics informed US refugee admissions policies, which were anchored in anticommunism, despite the fact that ideology was not part of the language of the UN Convention. With this new ideological criterion, overtly stated or otherwise, countries like the United States reintroduced an additional constraint that delimits the provision of status and protection only to certain types of the politically displaced, specifically, only to those fleeing left-wing and not right-wing persecution. In examining the US refugee resettlement programs for Hungarians and Cubans under the Eisenhower administration, the historian Anita Casavantes Bradford argues that the United States was motivated less by humanitarian concerns than by geopolitical aims to assert its moral obligation as the perceived leader of the free world and to affirm "Americans' belief in the superiority of their democratic-capitalist system."[33] A similar Cold War logic dictated US policies on asylum seekers from Central America that deny them refugee status, despite their having demonstrated fear as a result of targeted persecution and generalized violence.

Though the Refugee Act of 1980 that reaffirms the 1951 Convention definition of *refugee* divested US refugee policy of its ideological overtones and brought it into alignment with UN conventions and protocols, the US policy lacunae regarding asylum seekers from Latin America and the Caribbean and politicization of immigration and refugee policies persist in the post–Cold War years. Casavantes Bradford argues that in the case of Latin America, the United States's "historic biases against people of Latin American origin" produced an "immigration-averse public" that saw the "U.S. as vulnerable to being overrun by 'third world' immigrants," which accounts for the US objection to being a first country of asylum.[34]

This narrative is amplified in light of the en masse public migrations of Central American asylum seekers arriving at the US-Mexico border between 2017 and 2020, peaking at over 590,000 in 2019.[35] Under increasingly restrictive US immigration policies and Trump-era xenophobic policies that included draconian border patrol measures and virulent rhetoric about erecting a border wall, the US Immigration and Customs Enforcement (ICE) agency apprehended these asylum seekers to be sent back without sufficient efforts to adjudicate claims of fear (a potential violation of the 1951 Refugee Convention's principle of non-refoulement) or to be detained in centers throughout the southern and southwestern United States. In 2019, the US government forced approximately

60,000 displaced migrants seeking refuge in the United States to Mexico to wait out the asylum process.[36] By 2020, as a result of the combined effects of the coronavirus pandemic and increased repatriation to camps in Mexico, the number of ICE detentions declined to 177,391, though migrant deaths in detention rose from eight in the previous year to twenty-one.[37]

The Trump administration's anti-immigration stance was acutely reflected in its refugee policies, which significantly lowered the admission ceiling. In 2017, only 54,000 refugees were admitted, as compared to 85,000 in 2016 under the Obama administration. With COVID-19 public health concerns held up as justification, refugee admission was reduced to a historic low of 12,000 in 2020, with the ceiling set at 15,000 for 2021. The Joe Biden administration has expanded access to family-based immigration and extended eligibility for Temporary Protected Status to immigrants from Venezuela and Myanmar, providing them with time-limited permission to remain and work in the United States; it was a program that the Trump administration had sought to eliminate. Despite some positive movements, policies and practices regarding migrants at the US-Mexico border remain serious concerns for immigrant advocates. The Biden administration has vacillated on refugee issues. After initially stating that it would adhere to the 15,000 cap on refugee admission set by the Trump administration, the administration, after vigorous criticisms and pushbacks from refugee advocates, reaffirmed its commitment to raise the number of refugee admissions to 62,500 in 2021 and 125,000 in 2022 but not without first noting the challenges in meeting that goal.[38]

The recent "crisis" of public mass migrations and subsequent mass migrant detentions reveal two important truths about the nonhumanitarian US state. First, Central Americans' public insistence on entry into and protection from countries of "first" asylum have exposed the fragile facade of liberal humanitarianism touted by Western state governments and human rights agencies. According to a Council on Foreign Relations report:

> In early 2019, Trump declared a national emergency at the U.S. border with Mexico, allowing him to redirect funds from the Department of Defense to construct new border barriers. He had previously deployed thousands of active-duty troops to harden the southern border. Additionally, the administration has attempted to restrict the flow of migrants by tightening the U.S. asylum regime and negotiating deals with Mexico and the Northern Triangle countries that would allow U.S. authorities to send many asylum seekers back to those countries.[39]

Second, as an extension of the nonhumanitarian policy of the United States, the separation of immigrant children was and continues to be a strategy the government uses as deterrence against migrants seeking refuge in the country.[40] In 2018, then US president Donald Trump signed a "zero tolerance policy" to separate asylum-seeking families at the US-Mexico border, which further criminalized an asylum process that was already deemed in US policy and public discourse "illegal" immigration.

According to the Southern Poverty Law Center, the Trump administration and the US government ramped up child separation through a "pilot program" conducted in El Paso, Texas, in mid-2017, before the "zero tolerance policy" was implemented on May 7, 2018. Under this program, any adult who crossed the border without authorization and was considered a misdemeanor or first-time offender "was detained and criminally charged," including unauthorized adult entrants who arrived with young children; in those instances, the adults were charged and their accompanying children taken from them. Because the US government did not create pathways for reunification, many parents were unable to reunite with their children.[41] On June 15, 2018, the US Department of Human Services revealed that it had separated nearly 2,000 children from their parents or guardians between April 19 and May 31.[42] Since mid-2018, numerous reports have emerged concerning the separated children and the difficulties of reuniting with their parents or guardians, as well as the abject conditions of the detention centers temporarily housing the children. The increased apprehensions of unaccompanied children, along with the separation of accompanying children from family members on arrival and placement in different detention centers, constitute one of the many alarming measures of the Trump presidency. According to a 2019 Congressional Research Service report, unaccompanied children from Mexico make up 12 percent of those apprehended at the border, while those from the three Central American countries comprise a startling 85 percent.[43] By fall 2020, the number of detained children had reached nearly half a million, with reports of unaccompanied children having been detained longer than the seventy-two-hour limit.[44]

The inhumane treatment of Central American asylum seekers shows how these families and communities and, by extension, their children are racialized and regarded as threats to US national security.[45] Referencing the earlier US refusal of asylum for Nicaraguans, Salvadorans, Guatemalans, and Haitians fleeing US-backed authoritative regimes and war violence, opting instead to characterize them as "unauthorized entrants who request asylum as economic migrants seeking to enrich themselves at the expense of U.S. citizen workers," Casavantes Bradford argues that the "zero tolerance policy" is neither an unprecedented act nor inconsistent with American values.[46] The shift in Central American immigration is not a new pattern. According to a Pew Research report, immigration from Central America rose by 25 percent between 2007 and 2015, with 115,000 new immigrants arriving in 2014 alone.[47]

The focus on the current "crisis" distracts from the ways in which US policies concerning asylum seekers from Latin America through its southern border have historically been restrictive and contentious. The US conquest of northern Mexico in the Mexican-American War (1846–48) and the ongoing geopolitics of border making to bolster US state sovereignty structure the illegibility and unlivability of migrant lives across borders. Indeed, the passage of the 1965 Immigrant Act imposing an annual quota of 20,000 admissions per country, along with deportation policies and increased border security measures, criminalized migrants from Latin America as "illegals."

These ongoing detentions further expose the 1951 Convention's inability to adjudicate a variety of human rights violations and forms of persecution, violence, and fear that have since emerged or to encourage nation-states to comply with existing international laws pertaining to and extending beyond refugee protection. The workings of refugee law within liberal democracy reveal that the United States, despite its claims to the contrary, was never a humanitarian state to begin with. Refugees and immigrants became even more vilified as potential terrorist threats after the 2016 US presidential election and the January 27, 2017, executive order banning the citizens of seven Muslim countries from entering the United States.[48] As opposed to the more "benevolent narrative about the 'good' refugee as deserving of rescue, the current discourse shores up U.S. exceptionalism, promotes distrust toward refugees, and advocates the tightening of national borders."[49]

US policies regarding Central American asylum seekers not only reveal the limits of liberal humanitarianism, but further underscore the inherent shortcomings of an international protection regime that leaves unattended the histories of violence, such as settler colonialism, past and continuing imperialist interventions, and ongoing support of authoritarian regimes that produce refugee-engendering state violence and economic dispossession, which, in turn, implicate the United States and other countries of the Global North. As the "insurrectional politics" of mass public migration from Central American reveals (see chapter 2), waiting for humanitarian agencies that will never come to their rescue to determine their legal status is an untenable option.[50]

Conclusion

Recognized refugees are the most documented migrants because they are state-legitimated forced migrants whose displacements and movements are managed by government and humanitarian agencies. This recognition, however, often serves to obfuscate the state-sponsored violence that initially produced their fear and displacement. It is also a descriptor of the privileged status that legal and "good" migrants often hold, one that is bound up with legitimate claims to persecution and fear but is often deployed to distinguish refugees from undocumented immigrants and asylum seekers and migrants, who are deemed "illegal" and undeserving of rescue because their claims are not perceived as legitimate and whose asylum would perpetuate violence for the state and its citizens. Accordingly, CRS contends that both documented and undocumented constitute legal statuses. While the humanitarian regime establishes seeking asylum as a supposed "noncrime," the myriad policies that delineate who deserves rescue reveal otherwise.[51]

This chapter shows how the 1951 Convention's geopolitically and historically specific framing constitutes the law's inherent limitations. Analyzing different forms of displacement, internal conflict and environmental degradation, gender and sexual persecution, and Central American forced migrations, it argues that refugee law cannot account for the multiplicity and complexity of refugee-producing conditions and refugee claims. However, we do not simply lament the law and the nation-state's inability to do better. Instead, in the next chapter, we unravel the law's incapacities so as to underscore refugees' capacious and creative ways of seeking better conditions of living, even as they navigate colonial, state, structural, and legal violence.

2 A Refugee Critique of Fear

On Livability and Durability

We are living on the edge of hell. We have been waiting for so long for the day that the world would hear our voice. I hope it is today.

ZOHER, a Palestinian Syrian refugee

They leave their homeland in search of a new domicile in strange lands, flee within their own country or embark on the dangerous journey in rubber boots on the Mediterranean—always hoping for a better life, a life in dignity.

HOMI K. BHABHA, quoted in GABY REUCHER, "The Dignity of Refugees"

Refugees are the zombies of the world, the undead who rise from dying states to march or swim toward our borders in endless waves.

VIET THANH NGUYEN, "The Hidden Scars All Refugees Carry"

Chapter 1 demonstrates a critical refugee studies critique of refugee law's limitations through its very formation. This chapter illuminates the critical and creative ways refugees speak back to the law to insist on their humanity. Our argument is this: refugees and asylum seekers are aware of their relationship to the law and submit to its requirements intentionally whenever possible in the hope of attaining protection. As displaced peoples, they are fully cognizant of the inconsistent workings of the law, the intrusion of politics in its application, and the protective regimes' mandate to adjudicate and preclude claims of inclusion and redress. For some forcibly displaced communities, the acquisition of refugee status may not be their primary or singular desire but rather the last recourse when the more overarching yearning—for instance, the ability *to return* to their ancestral homeland for Palestinian refugees and the ability *to stay* for environmentally dislocated Pacific Islanders—has been obviated.[1] Cognizant of the law's restrictive provisions, refugees exercise their agency by navigating, negotiating, and at times circumventing existing legal, political, and definitional constraints.

This chapter addresses the absence of humanity, or rather the unequal differential humanity, extended to different people, whether through laws, practices, or humanitarian interventions. For example, when Colonel David H. E. Opfer, then US military attaché in Phnom Penh, referred to the accidental B52 bombing of a ferry town in Cambodia in 1970 as "no great disaster,"[2] he was not referring in absolute terms to the four hundred lives buried under the rubble of the flattened town but to the fact that these four hundred lives were *Cambodian* lives, disposable in a war that had already been relegated to a "sideshow," and hence of lesser worth and consequence than other "more human" lives. Along the same lines, when refugee law requires refugees to demonstrate their "well-founded fear" by reliving their victimization through detailed testimonies of explicit and extreme forms of violence, it is the idea of their victimhood rather than their personhood that shapes the representation of, discourse about, and policy responses to refugees. Good intentions notwithstanding, the push to elevate public concerns about refugees' plight invariably gives way to the overemphasis on numbers and statistics that reduces the refugee figure at best to an object of rescue, divested of their humanity.

With particular attention to Central American asylum seekers, queer refugees, and Palestinian refugees, this chapter considers the limits of UN resolutions relating to refugees and, by extension, of the law's inherent inability to fully and effectively adjudicate fear and violence. In particular, we are interested in the law's failure to account for *livability,* which we define as *an insistence on a better life that is not centered on fear but on humanity, dignity, and futurity.* As we elaborate below, livability, as a holistic and nuanced approach that encompasses the histories, memories, politics, physical life, and future of the forcibly displaced, extends not only beyond the present condition of fear, but beyond fear itself; it illuminates the ways in which refugees negotiate, reject, and creatively respond to the legal-political requirements to secure more than refuge and the right to live but the right to live fearlessly. In focusing on livability rather than eligibility, we argue for the importance of shifting the approach to refugee laws and policies beyond compliance "with internationally recognized *basic minimum* standards" and toward commitment to ensuring quality and dignity of life for the globally displaced.[3] While in this chapter we acknowledge the power of law to constitute reality, we also advance a Feminist Refugee Epistemology approach by looking to refugees' meaning-making practices, particularly poetry, to articulate not only their despairs but also their yearnings. Underscoring the importance of storytelling in its plurality, and with poetry—one of the few rhetorical tools available to migrants—as a creative and critical lens, this chapter redirects the gaze from statistics, disembodied policies, and macro analyses to refugee lifeworlds, especially facets that are often unseen and unacknowledged, where living happens across borders, where time exceeds the legal present, and where life is dignified.

From Fear to Livability

As established in chapter 1, states invariably interpret international refugee laws according to their perceived national security, economic, and cultural interests, denying many displaced people inclusion, goods, and services in the process. In the United States, anti-immigration rhetoric is often couched in terms of white injury that regularly casts white male middle-class citizens as the victims of immigration. In so doing, states co-opt and deploy what Nevzat Soguk calls the "language of fear" by manipulating it and turning it against migrants. In the current global landscape of rising right-wing extremism, the timeworn nativistic rhetoric that depicts migrants as an economic, cultural, and public health threat has been amplified by the vilification of asylum seekers as terrorists and a national security threat. In this context, many nation-states began to couch their rejection and detention of would-be refugees as efforts to eradicate terror and danger.[4] As an ACLU Immigrant Rights specialist concludes, "The Department of Justice's so-called 'war on terrorism' increasingly looks like a war on immigrants."[5] Refugees and asylum seekers are thus subjugated to state violence not only in the sending but also in the receiving context—by the very state in which they had sought refuge. As such, migrants are often subject to the double burden of fear: the fear that they themselves encountered in their home country, which led to their displacement, and the fear that they allegedly pose to the host country, which vilifies them as a threat.

In extreme instances, the political fabrication of threat—and by extension, of fear—moves beyond rhetoric and toward the actual attempt to eradicate the perceived threat. As an example, in 2002, capitalizing on the global War on Terror to accelerate its own internal war against ethnic Albanians, the Macedonian government conspired to kill seven Pakistani and Indian migrants who were on their way to Western Europe, charging them with collaborating with "Al Qaeda and ethnic Albanian rebels" to carry out attacks against the British, American, and German embassies.[6] As Nevzat Soguk notes, "'Macedonia's quest to join the war on terror' could be initiated this way, on migrant bodies seen and treated as bare lives whose killing or abuse did not necessarily constitute a crime in the minds of many."[7]

For Central American refugees and asylum seekers, whose numbers have soared since 2018 as large groups of people—including many women and children—moved by land across international borders toward the US-Mexico border, refugee law's collusion with the US asylum process produces and compounds their legal illegibility.[8] The US border patrol agents who meet the migrants at the US-Mexico border are but the first layer of a thick and, for most, impenetrable process of asylum seeking. The subjection of Central American migrants to state violence—experienced as the "terror . . . dispensed over papers and coffee cups, and under fluorescent lights"—is effectively rendered in the poem below, "The People vs. Us," by the Los Angeles–based Honduran poet and physician Felix Aguilar, which insists that in a context where "in just another day at work," lives can be lost, gained, or suspended in perpetual liminality, it is the state apparatus that is simultaneously the arbiter of justice and the dispenser of violence.

Do you waive your right
to a speedy trial?

La ley es la ley.
The law is the law.[9]

In this poem, Aguilar depicts, through the characters Jesús, the US public defender, and the immigration judge, the inverted nature of the asylum process. While Jesús, as an asylum seeker, is accused of "violating the law," it is in fact the law that is terrorizing him.

Terror is dispensed over
papers and coffee cups,
and under fluorescent lights.

While the indifferent public defender and the sneering judge practice and manipulate the law as part of their mundane workday, for Jesús and others like him, the words of the law "cut like dull knives" as they coerce asylum seekers to "waive" their rights in order to be considered for the attainment of rights. Jesús is ordered by the public defender "in accented Spanish" to "¡Diga si! (Say yes!)." The poem's title, "The People vs. Us," eerily captures the collective indictment of and lack of concern for Central American asylum seekers exhibited by refugee law and flouted by US citizens and the larger international community.

The language of fear is double-edged, embedded in a legal structure in which states expect refugees to demonstrate fear to gain entry but also regard them as those who are to be feared. Displaced people thus carry the fear of violence or the threat of it being enacted on their persons *and* the weight of the harm they allegedly pose to the state's citizen-subjects, which further endangers them. In her poem, "The United States Welcomes You," the US Poet Laureate Tracy K. Smith exposes the criminalizing process of testifying to fear before the law. Composed as a series of questions, the poem captures the brisk and protracted interrogation exacted against migrants seeking asylum in the United States.

> Why and by whose power were you sent?
> What do you see that you may wish to steal?
> . . . .
> Is this some enigmatic type of test? What if we
> Fail? How and to whom do we address our appeal?[10]

These rapid-fire questions convey the interrogator's a priori knowledge that asylum seekers are thieves with "dark bodies," sent by a competing political power "to steal" and "drink up all the light." And the questions, "what are you demanding / That we feel? Have you stolen something?," signal that asylum petitioners are not entitled to compassion, let alone justice. Smith's meticulous curation of fear in the poem thus captures what asylum seekers already know: they are intended to fail this test that criminalizes their being because their fear is unrecognizable in a political landscape that prioritizes the nation-state's fear of them. As the literary scholar Mai-Linh Hong exactingly explains, "Laws governing refugee protection and resettlement . . . are opaque and bewildering to navigate . . . because they were not meant to be navigated *by refugees*."[11] In other words, the law pertaining to refugees "works" because it produces and maintains the seeming dichotomy of the "language of fear" and the language of rescue. In compelling refugees to repeatedly attest to being fearful, the state is simultaneously coaching them to exhibit gratefulness for the space they have been allowed (see chapter 3).

At a more overarching level, the most critical pitfall of the existing refugee regime is that the aim of refugee law is truncated: to "address the problems refugees *pose,* not the problems refugees *face.*"[12] As indicated in chapter 1, critical refugee studies departs from the 1951 Convention definition of *refugee* whose restrictive legal and historical framing cannot account for the different and complex conditions that create refugees, including many emergent situations unanticipated or disregarded at the initial formulation of the UN refugee law. The 1951 Convention also fails to account for the historical continuum of violence and its persisting assault on people's everyday lived experiences. To shift this paradigm, we offer a refugee critique of the law that recenters refugee *livability* to name the capacious and bountiful ways of refugee living and lifeworlds that are complex in their physical, individual, communal, political, spiritual, and afterlife possibilities.

Focused on futurity, livability conveys what the anthropologist Lisa Stevenson describes as "the truth of the possible as opposed to the actual" that animates "a life that is very much 'beside itself.'"[13] In her work on suicide and care in the Inuit community, Stevenson poignantly asks, "How might we come to care for life that is constitutively beside itself, life that could never be fully itself?"[14] Leaning on Stevenson's insights, CRS conceptualizes refugee livability as the mundane, creative, and fantastic possibilities refugees live and dream about. These are the conditions and experiences of (un)livability that international refugee law overlooks and erases in its singular preoccupation with protecting only physical life, if that. As an example, for Vietnamese refugees, fear of communism was the basis of their claim for protection and a narrative that they have had to repeatedly recount during the long asylum application process, despite the painful memories that it evokes for many of them. And yet, as Thuy Vo Dang has shown, anticommunism has also come to function, for the refugees and their children, as a "cultural discourse" on war, loss, and displacement conducive to community building, to contesting historical forgetting, and to helping younger generations envision a future yet to come.[15] In short, for the US state, anticommunism is an indicator of the refugees' fear, required for asylum; for the refugees, anticommunism is an account of not only the used-to-bes but also the will-bes, necessary for community regeneration.

At the core of the concept of livability, then, is quality of life, as expressed through refugee storytelling and other self-produced narratives about displacement and exile, efforts to navigate fear and the law, and strategies of life (re)making. It animates the intention to live fearlessly, even with trauma and uncertainty. As the rest of the chapter demonstrates, refugee humanity, durability, and dignity make radical the insistence on quality refugee living and life (re)making.

Toward a Dignified Life

A key argument of this chapter is that the existing liberal humanitarian paradigm is unable to address and even actively invalidates claims made by refugees and asylum seekers, who have been forcibly displaced by the deleterious effects of settler colonialism, liberal militarized empire, and imperialism. Both policy and popular analyses of recent large-scale forced migration from Afghanistan, Syria, Sudan, and the Democratic Republic of Congo, among others, have largely ignored and aggressively discounted the longer histories of overlapping forms of violence levied against these countries by multiple Western forces. As with the case of Southeast Asian refugees whose experiences with overlapping histories of French colonialism and US militarism have been largely ignored, contemporary refugees of entangled injurious histories are often expected to exchange erasure of these historical and personal memories for rescue and resettlement eligibility. Against these forms of institutional erasure, our concept "refugee livability" takes seriously the claims of the displaced, which have been peripheralized by existing laws and by the pressure to articulate and perform fear only in ways that are legible to the liberal humanitarian system. In this section, we build on this concept by introducing the related concept "refugee dignity."

For asylum seekers who are queer and/or undocumented, organizing for asylum that centers refugee dignity means emphasizing the *everywhereness* of "differential statuses and mobilities."[16] In his generative analysis of the 2006 "A Day Without an Immigrant" boycott, Nicholas De Genova insists that the mobilization of undocumented migrants throughout the United States to publicly proclaim their collective presence—with the defiant slogan "¡Aquí Estamos, y No Nos Vamos!" (Here we are, and we're not leaving!)—should be read as a form of *queer* politics that unapologetically asserts their presence, everywhere. De Genova suggests that this radical politics of migrant presence—the refusal to be invisible—destabilizes the reverence for state power and the legitimacy of its immigration and border security regimes, producing new queer political actors who refuse to beg the state for their rights to a dignified life.[17] The 2006 "A Day Without an Immigrant" boycott thus centers queer approaches to livability and dignity, shifting the frame of migrant organizing away from the liberal humanitarian immigrant justice paradigm. In a similar example, Melissa Autumn White suggests that Julio Salgado's "I Am Undocuqueer" protest-art project foregrounds the "imperceptible presence" of migrants everywhere, disrupting the activism around the DREAM Act that differentiates between deserving and undeserving undocumented subjects.[18] Queer migrant activism thus incorporates "seemingly divergent strategies" to remake space, a process of "respatializing" that challenges nation-state territorialities and normative gender and sexual identities that confine "desire, holding it in place."[19] As such, remaking space points to the idea of offering sanctuary as a radical form of welcome for vulnerable and targeted populations.

Understood within the framework of a queer politics of migration, the willfully public Central American migrant caravans that have traveled from El Salvador, Guatemala, and Honduras to seek asylum in the United States since 2017 demand "accompliceship" from Americans and the international community to stand against the law by radically welcoming families, unaccompanied children, and queer and trans migrants.[20] The mass public migrations, which involve crossing multiple borders and rejecting victimhood and surreptitiousness, constitute what Soguk calls "insurrectional politics," whereby the migrants capture borders, compelling citizens within those state boundaries to aid their efforts to (re)claim dignity. In explaining the surge of migrants to the US-Mexico border, a Council on Foreign Relations report states, "Unlike past waves of migrants, in which most attempted to cross illegally without detection, migrants from the Northern Triangle often surrender to U.S. border patrol agents to claim asylum."[21] Because the US state has consistently refused to recognize Central Americans as refugees, categorizing them instead as undocumented, the migrants' public proclamations to seek protection from "violent assaults, oppressive extortions, and murdered loved ones"[22] turn them into *insurrectional refugees* who expose the territorial vulnerability of the United States.[23] The "mass" and public nature of the Central American migrant caravans reflects the asylum seekers' repeatedly stated fear of gang violence, itself an extension of the poverty, crime, and environmental disasters that have been generated in part by long-term US economic and military incursions in the region. That fear, rather than invoking humanitarian sympathy, is appropriated by the US state as *its own* fear, one that necessitates the denial of migrant protection in the name of national safety and security.

A queer politics of migration that prioritizes migrants' dignity leads to an abolitionist approach to sanctuary, away from the liberal appropriation of sanctuary policies and municipal territorializing. A. Naomi Paik has argued that abolitionism can work on multiple fronts to undo capitalist exploitation, borders, policing, caging, and patriarchy.[24] To elaborate, a practice and politics of sanctuary that is imbued with the Black radical tradition of abolition acknowledges that Indigenous displaced peoples' insistence on a dignified life is multifaceted, encompassing the right to stay in their homeland but also the right to leave and to return. For undocumented queer asylum seekers, the right to stay in the United States as a first asylum country not only privileges the physicality of security and geopolitical access but also humanizes racial, gender, and sexual identity, muting its "immutable" fixity in the law.

In sum, non-UN-recognized refugees who are compelled to escape and cross borders despite legal and state sanctions are in fact enacting the radical politics of refugees to move and live fearlessly. In doing so, they recuperate the radical potential of mobility in forced migrations, removed from liberal ideas about rescue and freedom. As Antonia Maldonado, an asylum seeker from Honduras waiting in the makeshift Matamoros refugee camp in Mexico, explains, "I just want to live with dignity. I'm not asking for riches."[25] Such pursuit of safety with dignity—of livability—cannot be adjudicated on the singular criterion of fear. The only durable solution is a durable life.

"We Teach Life, Sir": Palestinian Refugees, Durable Life-Making, and the Failures of International Law

While international law orients itself to refugee fear, some refugee fears are made illegible precisely as a result of the demands of international law. In this section, we show how Palestinian refugees wishing to expose their day-to-day realities and fears as a result of Israeli settler colonialism have had to muzzle their fears. Therein lies their predicament: for Palestinian refugees to be seen and heard by the international community, they have to be quiet and invisible about the cause of their displacement. We discuss how Palestinian refugees have interrogated the assumption of redemption and legibility by international laws and exposed the horrifying conditions that have produced their protracted displacement. Specifically, we show how Palestinian refugee poets narrate the materiality of ongoing violence—using their voices as testimony to that which has been silenced in international law and popular media—while also insisting on a better and dignified life, one that cannot be reducible to "bare life."[26]

In 1948, over 800,000 Palestinians were displaced from historic Palestine by the settler colonial project of Zionism, producing the world's largest and most protracted refugee exodus. Zionism was a European project that sought to "reunite" the European Jewish diaspora on Indigenous Palestinian lands at the height of European anti-Semitism. To justify the violent expulsion of Palestinians, Zionist discourse constructed Palestinian lands as an undeveloped wonderland for Zionist Jews seeking Jewish "return" to the "Land of Israel."[27] Palestinians name 1948 the year of the Nakba (Arabic for "catastrophe"), which involved European settler colonialism, genocidal massacres, dispossession, displacement, degradation of the natural environment, and demolition of home and homeland.

Although the Nakba occurred just three years before the 1951 Convention, the United Nations created a distinct regime for displaced Palestinians that consisted of two bodies: the United Nations Relief Works Agency (UNRWA) and the United Nations Conciliation Commission on Palestine (UNCCP). The UNRWA oversaw services for Palestinians, who were deemed to be "in need," and "inherited" nearly one million refugees from previous refugee agencies. It defines refugees as "groups and categories of vulnerable persons designated on the basis of need for services." The UNRWA's definition, with its focus on "need for services," would contradict the 1951 Convention's emphasis on fear, effectively excluding Palestinian refugees from what would become the universal category of refugee. In these ways, refugee law effectively occludes ongoing Israeli settler colonialism and militarism because the UNRWA's emphasis on those "in need" is not formally tied to the 1951 Convention's notion of "well-founded fear." The UNCCP's attempts to seek "durable solutions" to Palestinian displacement included repatriation, resettlement, restitution, and compensation based on the unconditional principle of refugee choice.[28] However, Israel has continually opposed repatriation and tightened its regime of control.[29] While the UNCCP continues to operate, "its role is no more than functionary—a symbol of international responsibility to the refugees, and a sad reminder of unfulfilled commitments."[30] Together, these two organizations—the UNRWA and the UNCCP—reveal the limitations of refugee law's discourse, as well as the failure to address the root cause of the ongoing production of Palestinian refugees: Israel's settler colonialism and military occupation. While the UNRWA provides some temporary services, Palestinians residing in refugee camps in frontline Arab countries continue to be undocumented, with only Jordan offering citizenship to Palestinians. And yet Palestinians globally still insist on the Right of Return.

Today, Palestinian refugees are in their seventh generation of displacement. An estimated 1.3 million Palestinian refugees live in the Gaza Strip (hereafter Gaza), where they are registered as UNRWA refugees. Gaza, the size of Philadelphia, is one of the most densely populated places in the world, with a population of 1.9 million, the majority (1.3 million) of whom are refugees from Palestinian villages that were depopulated or exterminated in 1948. Because of the denial of the durable solution of repatriation, Gaza's refugees are not only excluded in international law and denied the Right of Return to their ancestral homes; they also live under a military occupation and blockade that seals Gaza via air, land, and sea, leading many to characterize Gaza as the largest open-air prison in history.

In December 2008, Israel instigated a twenty-two-day military assault on Gaza that killed 1,400 Palestinians and destroyed civilian infrastructures in the name of counterterrorism, launching three hundred air strikes on the besieged enclave during the first week alone. On the eighth day, Israel followed with a ground invasion supported by artillery fire and fighter jets supplied by the United States. Most insidious, however, was Israel's indiscriminate use of a chemical weapon called white phosphorous—an extremely dangerous and destructive compound that penetrates muscle and bone, causing irreparable damage to internal organs and death by implosion. More recently, in May 2021, the Israeli air and sea forces carried out an eleven-day military attack on Gaza, the fourth since 2008. According to the Palestinian Ministry of Health, the attacks killed 254 Palestinians, including 66 children, 39 women, and 17 elderly, and injured 1,948 others. In addition, the missile attacks forced about 120,000 Palestinians across Gaza to flee their homes; many sought refuge in schools belonging to the UNRWA.[31] Gaza's refugees thus continue to be subjected to a quartet of oppressions: forcible displacement, total containment, humanitarian crisis, and military occupation.

In spite of this terrifying reality, Gaza's refugees are the ones who continue to be placed on trial. Soon after Israel's 2008 assault on Gaza, Rafeef Ziadeh, while working as a media spokesperson for a coalition of organizers, was asked by a journalist, "Don't you think it would all be fine if you stopped teaching your children how to hate?" Ziadeh, a third-generation Palestinian refugee whose family was expelled from Palestine during the 1948 Nakba, addresses this violent encounter in the form of a poem, "We Teach Life, Sir," which went viral within days.[32] The poem's opening lines encapsulate Ziadeh's fury.

> Today, my body was a TV'd massacre.
> Today, my body was a TV'd massacre that had to fit into sound-
> bites and word limits.
> Today, my body was a TV'd massacre that had to fit into sound-
> bites and word limits filled enough with statistics to counter
> measured response.

In these opening lines, Ziadah passionately exposes how Palestinians are often asked to prove their fearfulness and victimhood while maintaining a composed and palatable image for Western media. The journalist's seemingly innocuous question reveals the layers of silence and abandonment so characteristic of international law and its failures. The anguished phrase, "Today, my body was a TV'd massacre," reveals the constraints of legibility in which Palestinians must adapt a limited number of "sound-bites" to prove that they, indeed, live in fear. With her massacre on televised display, Ziadah is expected to emit carefully measured syllables and just "enough statistics" to "prove" her worthiness and humanity without overburdening the viewer, even as "bombs drop over Gaza."

> And I perfected my English and I learned my UN resolutions.
> But still, he asked me, Ms. Ziadah, don't you think that every-
>   thing would be resolved if you would just stop teaching so
>   much hatred to your children?
> Pause.

She arms herself by perfecting her English and memorizing "UN resolutions"—strategies to quell skeptics and blunt allegations of falsehoods, the "measured response." And yet she is still met with speculation and questioned about Palestinians' always already pathological proclivity to teach "so much hatred." So Ziadah tries harder to prove her humanity through the very regimes of law that have effaced her pain: "I give them UN resolutions and statistics and we condemn and we deplore and we reject."

> And these are not two equal sides: occupier and occupied.
> And a hundred dead, two hundred dead, and a thousand dead.
> And between that, war crime and massacre, I vent out words and
>   smile "not exotic", "not terrorist".

Throughout the poem, Ziadah tells of being barraged with demands "to give us a story," "a human story," one that is "not political" and that does not mention the terms "apartheid" and "occupation." At one point, the journalist (referred to as "sir" and "they") implores Ziadah to depoliticize her story so that he can *help* her, reminiscent of the many humanitarian offers that have failed to account for Palestinian refugees: "You have to help me as a journalist to help you tell your story which is not a political story." Of course, the insistence on not being political in order to be seen as human deserving of assistance is itself a form of erasure. On the one hand, Palestinians' right to refugee status is made impossible by an international discourse that is fixated on refugee fear; on the other, the terrifying conditions that lead to their very fears must be muted in order for them to gain any sound bites about their plight. This occlusion cannot reconcile with the repetitive statement that the narrator's body is a televised massacre: "Today my body was a TV'd massacre." The use of repetition digs up and exposes the buried reality of ongoing settler colonialism and militarized violence, diverting the focus, even for a moment, from the oblivious journalist seeking the vacuous story to the Palestinian's embodied experiences of terror. In this way, Ziadeh's poem illustrates a form of refugee *Sumud* (Arabic for "steadfastness") in the face of penetrating fear: she bears witness to a bodily violence that she experiences while also exposing this violence by mastering the discourse of the legal apparatus and becoming proficient in the art of broadcast.

Amplifying the material conditions of fear, Ziadeh's poem exposes the limitations of international law by critiquing the very regimes of protection that have rendered Palestinians' fear illegible—most notably, the United Nations. Ziadeh's proclamation that she had learned her UN resolutions suggests that international law is a discourse that she mobilizes to affirm the legibility of her people's fear but to which she has no personal attachment. Indeed, she adopts a cynical tone toward international law, explicitly challenging the relevance of the legal apparatus.

And let me just tell you, there's nothing your UN resolutions have
    ever done about this. And no sound-bite, no sound-bite I
    come up with, no matter how good my English gets, no
    sound-bite, no sound-bite, no sound-bite, no sound-bite will
    bring them back to life.
No sound-bite will fix this.

Here the rhythmic echo, "no sound-bite," challenges the liberal assumption that if the right people and organizations in the Anglophone West know about their suffering, Palestinian refugees will be protected. As the Palestinian legal scholar Noura Erakat has shown, no judicial interventions have resolved the inadequacies of international refugee laws and laws of war that continue to permit the killing and destruction of Israel's military offensives in Gaza.[33] As such, Ziadeh's poem—and poetry more generally—becomes the refugees' medium for placing international law and public broadcasts on trial for negligence.

Ziadeh's poem is most notable for its repetition of "We teach life, sir," which occurs at the end of the poem.

We teach life, sir.
We teach life, sir.
We Palestinians wake up every morning to teach the rest of the
    world life, sir.

What does it mean that Palestinians "teach life" in the very moment that they are barraged with deadly bombs? According to Loubna Qutami and Omar Zahzah, Palestinians "invent life where life is constantly under attack," such that "if Palestinians can teach anything to the world, anything at all, it would be these techniques of creating, inventing and salvaging life where it is never meant to exist."[34] As teachers of life in the face of legal failure, Gaza's refugees effectively transcend the requisite performativity of fear, choosing instead to bear witness to life even as it is lived on a thread. While "durable solutions" have proven to be an unfulfilled promise due to the denial of the Right of Return, Ziadeh's poem points to the practices of *durable life-making*—the daily practices of bravely enacting *livability* in the context of the terrifying realities of material violence and discursive erasure. In these ways, "We teach life, sir" attends to the ways that refugees, even while afraid, navigate through fear through their insistence on life—on livability.

For Palestinian refugees in Gaza, the failure of international law to recognize the Palestinian definition of fear and its exclusion of Palestinians from universal refugee protections continue now into the seventh generation. The UN's decision to exclude Palestinians from the "universal" happened by and through the establishment of a regime of protection. Over time, the most significant durable solution of repatriation to ancestral homelands vis-à-vis the Right of Return was severed from the refugee definition.[35] Rafeed Ziadeh's poem "We Teach Life, Sir" challenges the hegemony of the law as well as the liberal notion that being saved is a matter of being seen—by exposing the ways that Palestinian refugees in Gaza are unseeable in the eyes of the law even as their bodies are subjected to televised massacres that are widely circulated in social media. In spite of this persistent failure of international law, Ziadeh's poem reveals the everyday practices of durable life-making—such as bearing witness to Palestinian fear, mastering the legal conventions to assert Palestinian humanity, and insisting that Palestinians are teachers of life—recasting Palestinian refugees in Gaza as survivors of legitimate fear while also transcending international law's grip on their legibility. In doing so, Ziadeh, alongside other Palestinian truth tellers, calls attention to the ways in which Palestinian refugees have bravely insisted on livability, exposing the failures of international law and its regimes of "protection."

Critical Redefinition of "the Refugee"

Departing from the 1951 Convention definition of "the refugee," which is preoccupied with "fear and persecution," critical refugee studies illuminates and underscores the centrality of livability and durability of refugee life, foregrounding how people who experience refugee conditions make and live their lives—their concerns, perspectives, knowledge production, and global imaginings. In so doing, CRS illuminates the underrepresented lived worlds of displacement and/or statelessness that cannot be reduced to dispossession or abjection but are affectively rich, complex, and multidimensional. Of particular note, CRS recognizes that "refugee" is a status that the statutory powers of international and state laws do not have sole and privileged authority to determine. In place of the limited and limiting language in the 1951 UN Convention on Refugees, CRS offers the following redefinition of the refugee.

> Refugees are human beings forcibly displaced within or outside of their land of origin as a result of persecution, conflict, war, conquest, settler/colonialism, militarism, occupation, empire, and environmental and climate-related disasters, regardless of their legal status. Refugees can be self-identified and are often unrecognized within the limited definitions proffered by international and state laws.[36]

As elaborated in chapter 1, while legal status in the eyes of states, interstate entities, and nongovernmental organizations undeniably has an impact on refugees materially and ideologically, a key premise of CRS is the need to expose the ways that existing epistemologies and institutions reproduce the very conditions that created, in Edward Said's words, these "herds of innocent and bewildered people." For in the production of these "herds" is a simultaneous critique of a world order that permits such outrages and the uninterrogated reaffirmation of that order.

In positing that it is the existence of the globally displaced that provides the clue to a new social order in which all refugees are treated and embraced as fellow human beings with all fundamental rights and privileges, CRS moves beyond the legally designated definition of refugees that is premised on "fear and persecution," offering instead an expanded and nuanced definition of "the refugee" that includes all "human beings forcibly displaced within or outside of their land of origin . . . , regardless of their legal status."[37] In short, CRS's redefinition departs from the limited definitions proffered by international and state laws by insisting that "refugees can be self-identified" and that *moving away from the legal definition of refugee allows for refugee livability.*

While it may have been easier to conceptualize a theoretical shift for redefining the refugee, the process of delineating the refugee's position and positionality—from object to subject (as one who enacts) and agent—has been and will be challenging. Consistent with how we have conceptualized refugee livability, our redefinition of "the refugee" is an example of FRE as it accounts for the moments of living that can enhance our recognition of each other without the state, policies, and human rights. That recognition allows us to address refugees and ourselves with courage and even grace.

Toward that vision, the Critical Refugee Studies Collective has culled a list of critical vocabulary that is commonly used to describe refugees and their conditions but has reclaimed their meanings and imbued them with a refreshed political urgency.[38] As an example, Victor Bascara reanimates the term "empire," which itself has seen critical intervention from the various interdisciplines of American studies, ethnic studies, and gender and sexuality studies, by way of a reading of the Somali British poet Warsan Shire's poem "Home." Citing the poem's critical line, "No one leaves home unless / home is the mouth of a shark," Bascara insists that "empire" is that shark and that refugee experiences, epistemologies, and expressions make that shark unmistakable, including the mouth that is the home one has been forced to abandon and the rest of the shark's body that is fed by that mouth. In the latter part of the poem, Shire asks, "look at what they've done to their own countries, / what will they do to ours?" As the question is set up, it is likely spoken by a racist xenophobe and directed at the embodied, corrupting threat of the refugee figure.

> dark, with their hands out
> smell strange, savage—
> look at what they've done to their own countries,
> what will they do to ours?

A critical refugee studies method of reading makes it possible for us to consider what it might mean for the dash after "savage" to indicate a break, a shift to another's interiority. That is to say, what would it mean if the refugee asked that question? This very interrogation is precisely what may be happening in this poem that adamantly centers the refugee. Recognizing this perspective would mean that the refugee would be recognized as a critical subject and not just an object—not just a "running. beaten. raped. starved. pitied. dirty. Savage" object of empire's latest mission to shape the world in its image.[39]

Conclusion

In tandem with chapter 1, this chapter interrogates how refugee law adjudicates refugee claims based on a temporally and spatially demarcated conceptualization of fear; refugees whose experiences of fear diverge from these parameters have a difficult time availing themselves of the law's protections. Moreover, many refugees face a double burden in regard to fear. They must successfully communicate their fear of violence to the receiving state to gain asylum *and*, simultaneously, assuage that state's fears of them as perceived violent intruders. At the same time, refugees who are Indigenous, internally displaced, queer, or undocumented often want more than asylum; they demand decolonization, return of land, the right to return home, the right to stay, and demilitarization, among other things, from the international community and state governments. Refugees' rights claims thus reveal the law's inadequate coverage at best and malevolent disregard at worst. In advancing a refugee critique of the law, critical refugee studies argues for refugee livability that is beyond the fear and the psychic value of life as defined by the law and toward the valuing of living that is there but not seen. Livability names the fearless possibilities of living, in its claims of the right to return, to stay, and to move audaciously—to be present everywhere. Livability thus shifts the burden of proving fear from refugees and onto the state. On these terms, the truth of the law is but one aspect of refugees' lives such that their ease of living is beside the law.

3 *A Refugee Critique of Humanitarianism*

On Ungratefulness and Refusal

I would really like the native-born to think about what's going on in the psyche of these newcomers and what they might need. I think the biggest thing they would need, aside from the shelter and food, is love and dignity.

DINA NAYERI

Humanitarianism, at its best, connotes a "politics of care for the needy, marginalized, and displaced" and "a basic bundle of protections for shelter, food, and medical care in moments of crisis."[1] However, as many scholars have established, despite the dedication, good intentions, and important work of many humanitarian agents, humanitarian discourses and practices of benevolence, while more subtle than overt racism, uphold patriarchal and neocolonial relations of power and systems of meaning and representation that bolster the unequal relationship between refugees and the humanitarians who claim to save them.[2] From the perspective of the refugees, this unequal relationship is most evident in rescue narratives in which refugees are expected to exhibit gratefulness for the space they have been allowed and the aid they have received. While chapters 1 and 2 examine how international refugee law demands proof of fear from those seeking safety, this chapter analyzes how humanitarian agencies and agents expect a display of gratitude from those who have been "rescued." In her aptly titled book *The Ungrateful Refugee,* which weaves her own story with the stories of other refugees and asylum seekers in recent years, the Iranian American writer Dina Nayeri unflinchingly insists that refugees and asylum seekers should not have to "spend the rest of our days in grateful ecstasy, atoning for our need."[3] Heeding Nayeri's clarion call for refugee refusal, this chapter relies on refugee stories—both fiction and creative nonfiction—penned by refugee authors to offer a *refugee critique* of humanitarianism, delineating how humanitarianism originates from and reproduces unequal power relationships and how refugees experience and subvert this power differential. The goal, as always, is to approach refugee life with nuance, care, and complexity—to mark the ways that refugees (re)present themselves not in grateful deference to the host countries but always in relation to their own need for livability, safety, and dignity.

Refugees as Subjects of Humanitarianism

The Refugee Story: Crisis-Rescue-Gratitude

Crisis-rescue-gratitude constitutes the long-standing triad of popular accounts of refugee lives. Like any good story line, the established refugee story, circulated liberally through multiple media outlets, official pronouncements, and everyday conversations, relies on a narrative arc: in act 1, the refugee is introduced as the victim of *crises* produced by faraway tragedies (see chapter 2); in act 2, the refugee is *rescued* by humanitarian organizations and citizens of

Global North nations; and in act 3, the refugee is prodded to profess eternal *gratitude* as tribute to their rescuers. Gratitude is thus the requisite closure—the resolution—of the refugee story plot. Without the gratitude ending, the refugee story would leave the reader—in this case, citizens of the host nation—unsatisfied, confused, and even angry. Accordingly, displaying appropriate gratefulness is a lesson repeatedly drilled into refugees. As Mai-Linh Hong maintains, the "[refugee's] labor will include gratitude."[4] Nayeri, who came to the United States from Iran as a child refugee along with her mother and brother, recounts how she learned early on to show her thanks: "If I failed to stir up in myself enough gratefulness, or if I failed to properly display it, I would *lose* all that I had *gained*." [5]

Nayeri's account of gratefulness—with its evocation of losses and gains—indexes the outsized impact of humanitarian narratives that depict refugee lives only in terms of losses and their resettlement in Western countries only in terms of gains. As refugee studies scholars and refugee writers have documented, "The trauma discourse and the pathologization of refugees is the most common reaction to the presence of refugees in Western arrival countries."[6] In an article on the economies of race and rescue of young African refugees, Sunčica Klaas posits that American refugee discourse tends to associate the "condition of refugeeness with child-like helplessness and innocence."[7] In this white paternalistic representational frame, "adoptable" refugees are malleable ones—capable of assimilating into the US national family and body politic through proper (white) parenting and guidance. The Rwandan American author Clemantine Wamariya, who fled the Rwandan massacre as a child with her older sister, Claire, details their differing resettlement experiences: Wamariya, still young enough to be malleable, lived with the Thomas family in a fancy suburb; her sister, married with kids, "work[ed] full-time as a maid, cleaning two hundred hotel rooms a week."[8] As Wamariya explains, "Unlike me, Claire was not a child when we got resettled in the United States, so nobody sent her to school or took her in or filled her up with resources—piano lessons, speech therapists, cheerleading camp."[9] But malleability, as a precondition of care, has its costs: Wamariya "was whoever anybody wanted me to be";[10] in contrast, Claire "refused to think . . . that anybody was better or more important than she was."[11]

The tendency to infantilize refugees is vividly captured in Americans' fixation on orphaned child refugees. Refugee war orphans, rescued from their "ravaged" native countries and whisked to "safety" on US shores, are popular subjects of humanitarianism in US immigration and refugee discourse—from British war orphans fleeing World War II London to unaccompanied Cuban children and teenagers escaping Fidel Castro's government to children orphaned or displaced by the Korean War to toddlers evacuated from the Vietnam War in the days before the fall of Saigon.[12] In the late 1990s and early 2000s, the US public was notably fascinated with the Lost Boys of Sudan, a large group of child refugees of Nuer and Dinka ethnicity who were displaced or orphaned during the Second Sudanese War (1983–2005). According to Klaas, the boys' compelling testimonies of dislocation, trauma, and resilience were widely circulated, amplified, and fetishized via documentaries, editorials, and broadcasts, as well as blockbuster movies, novels, and autobiographies. The Lost Boys' perceived innocence and hopefulness, which positioned them as damaged minors in need of "white humanitarian care,"[13] coupled with their exotic African blackness, stole the heart of the American people and public officials, prompting the Clinton administration to permit some 3,600 to resettle in the United States.[14] In short, the boys' eligibility for help and resettlement hinged on their recognition as "innocent *children*," even when most reached the United States as young men in their early twenties.[15]

The "white embrace" of child/infantilized refugees thus iconizes "children's vulnerability as quintessential refugee suffering"[16] and establishes "orphanhood"—that is, the condition of being without familial but also without national, cultural, and spiritual baggage—as a requirement for the bestowing of care and protection. However, without the requisite innocence and vulnerability, child refugees, too, become vilified trespassers. As Anita Casavantes Bradford argues, the US government's vilification of the influx of Central American migrant children, who traveled from Central America to the Mexico-US border in highly publicized migrant caravans that commenced in 2017, is due in large part to the fact that these youngsters, along with their parents, "have demonstrated desire, autonomy and resourcefulness in getting to the U.S. by themselves." For many Americans, their agency and visibility elicit distrust and anger because "[Americans'] notion of children's rights depends on a definition of children as dependent and as victims."[17] Such notions infantilize refugees by hinging their eligibility for assistance and resettlement on their ability to demonstrate their defenselessness and neediness rather than on the specificities of their histories of dislocation. As such, US humanitarian care on behalf of the uprooted is most often relegated to the individual or nonprofit sphere, with private and familial responsibility replacing collective, political action.[18] Within this racial configuration and privatized structure of refuge, the refugee victim is belittled and isolated, forever indebted to the resettlement state and its citizens for the bestowed "gift of freedom."[19]

The International Refugee Regime: Humanitarianism in Practice/Practicing Humanitarianism

The construction of refugees as in need of white humanitarian aid was consolidated in the last decades of the twentieth century when a new moral economy, centered on humanitarian reason, emerged as Western states instituted an international refugee regime with dual and at times competing goals: to regulate populations flows in order to safeguard their own sovereignty; and, secondarily, to coordinate efforts to protect refugees.[20] The tensions between the competing goals of repression and compassion, with compassion articulated as a *gift* to refugees rather than a recognition of their rights, generate refugee humanitarian narratives that are largely restricted to crises, suffering, and fear (see chapter 2), omitting refugees' rich layered lives in the process.[21]

But humanitarianism is not only a discourse; it is also a form of governing that involves an international refugee regime of nongovernmental organizations (NGOs), international agencies, states, and individuals. Nigel Hatton uses the term "global humanitarians" to name the constellation of global elites—international lawyers, judges, NGO workers, philanthropists, doctors, educators, corporatists, journalists, and politicians educated primarily in institutions in western and northern Europe, North America, and Australia—who work in humanitarian governance. Through their memoirs, speeches, human rights reports, internal memos, marketing campaigns, covenants, declarations, and other communiqués, these Western elites cumulatively strengthen and reify the "widely held understanding of humanitarian assistance as a *gift* from the elite Western provider to the poor developing world recipient."[22] Hatton argues that this "performance of superiority,"[23] "in which moral responsibility . . . is based on pity rather than the demand for justice,"[24] leaves the victim/survivor routinely unheard in the international system. Along the same lines, Jennifer Hyndman calls attention to the widespread humanitarian convention of configuring refugees as masses rather than as people: "These groups are often dematerialized into refugee statistics or homogenized and silenced under the rubric of voiceless refugees." Hyndman argues that "this strange evocation of charitable humanity" constitutes a form of "*semio-violence,* a representational practice that purports to speak for others but at the same time effaces their voices."[25] As Hatton explains, "The inability to speak with the victim, stranger, or refugee present in equal status and recognition is a central problem of the global peace and justice system, impacting the instruments and personnel of the United Nations, the UN Refugee Agency, and the International Criminal Court, the permanent court anchoring the international justice system."[26] It is important to note that in his statement, Hatton attributes speechlessness—the failure to speak—to the global humanitarians, not the refugees, who, as he argues, practice "nuanced and deafening speech acts."[27]

Western technologies of rescue also offer refugees "salvation" at the price of community loss, cultural uprooting, and forced assimilation, sustained by uneven relations of power. In her study of displaced Cambodians, Aihwa Ong recounts that a constellation of aid agencies—including the American Refugee Committee, OXFAM, Médecins sans Frontières, and Catholic Charities— assumed responsibility for training the refugees in the skills and attitudes they will need to become citizens of Western countries. As "agents of compassionate domination," relief workers, while providing much-needed assistance, reorganized the refugees' moral sense of who they were to become by "introduc[ing] specific technologies of governing that orient and shape the everyday behavior of refugees (usually from the less-developed world), transforming them into particular kinds of modern human beings (bound for Western liberal democracies)."[28] Cambodian refugees thus learned how to become new kinds of neoliberal subjects, resulting in "a radical break from Cambodian cultural autonomy as refugees came to rely on volags [voluntary agencies] for their everyday needs."[29]

Founded in December 1950, the United Nations High Commissioner of Refugees (UNHCR) is the world's lead humanitarian agency with the mandate and authority to protect and assist refugees, forcibly displaced communities, and stateless people.[30] The United Nations established the UNHCR to help states carry out their responsibilities to refugees but routinely presented themselves as "apolitical" and "humanitarian" to signal their recognition of sovereignty's principle of noninterference. In the period following World War II, humanitarianism became a "potent force,"[31] at times functioning as a "colonialism of compassion"[32] or a form of "refugee love" on behalf of sovereign states.[33] However, in the post–Cold War years, as eruptions of violence that precipitate major refugee flows—from Rwanda, Somalia, Iraq, Syria, Ethiopia, Afghanistan and more—increasingly take place intranationally rather than internationally, powerful would-be receiving states began to dodge legal obligations to asylum seekers by framing their displacement as the product of sectarian or ethnic conflicts rather than of histories of colonialism, imperialism, and militarism instigated by global superpowers in the region.[34] Moreover, depicting large-scale refugee displacements as "regional and international security risks," the international community trumpets containment of refugee flows and outsources the management of the "refugee problem" to multinational humanitarian organizations like the UNHCR.[35] As a consequence, the UNHCR's humanitarian work in the post–Cold War era becomes a deeply politicized process of balancing the needs of displaced persons against the security agenda of Western liberal states.

Funding patterns circumscribe the UNHCR's rhetorical and policy responses to displacement. As the agency is funded primarily on a voluntary basis by donor governments, it has to respond to the geopolitical, economic, and security concerns of the donor states, which often stipulate the use and location of their donations.[36] Tethered to fundraising concerns, the UNHCR has moved from engaging in planning, strategy, and knowledge production with refugees and activists and their communities networks to shaping the agency's policies with donors in mind. As Hyndman succinctly summarizes, government donors are the UNHCR's main clients; refugees and displaced people are its disenfranchised recipients.[37] The UNHCR's $1 billion private sector fundraising strategy for 2018–25 demonstrates the importance of fundraising experience and expertise. A UNHCR advertisement for a fundraiser details the responsibilities of the position: "Contribute to the development of fundraising strategies and products for diverse fundraising activities that serve to recruit and retain loyal individual donors, moving them through a donor journey that builds a lasting connection with UNHCR in order to maximize lifetime value and return on investment."[38] As the leading humanitarian donor in the world, the European Union, with a total budget of €2 billion in humanitarian aid in 2020,[39] has an outsized role in controlling UNHRC policy, which should be informed instead by a global citizenry. As such, humanitarian assistance will be largely anchored in the protection of nations of the European Union, which strategically links the functions of its two global aid departments—the Department of European Civil Protection and Humanitarian Aid Operations and the Department of Migration and Home Affairs—to safety at home. In this scenario, the life of refugees is situated structurally in contestation with the safety of the European citizen.

Once the UNHCR embraced the premise that internal sectarian conflicts, not Western military empires, precipitate massive refugee flows in the post–Cold War era and that these flows trigger regional instability and challenge "human security,"[40] it gradually dropped the noninterference principle and began to intrude in the domestic affairs of refugee-producing countries in an effort to stem "the root causes of refugee flows."[41] Repatriation also became a priority. Beginning in the mid-1980s and accelerating after the Cold War, as most displaced peoples were from and in the Global South, the UNHCR responded to states' desire for refugees to return home as soon as possible by intervening in repatriation decisions. In the 1990s, for example, it encouraged refugee returns under less than ideal conditions—including the forced repatriation of Vietnamese refugees in Southeast Asia to Việt Nam, Rohingya in Bangladesh to Myanmar, and Somalis in Kenya to Somalia—at times by overselling its ability to monitor the return and reintegration.[42] As the executor of repatriation programs, the UNHCR's interference holds sway and worsens precarity for refugees.

The shift away from absolute standards regarding the desire by refugees to repatriate given their assessment of the situation in the home country toward a comparative evaluation by agency officials regarding whether refugees would be more secure at home or in the camps has the direct implication of privileging the agency's knowledge claims over those offered by refugees.[43]

The UNHCR also abets donor states in the Global North by brokering the system of global refugee management, dubbed "the Grand Compromise," in which states in the Global South host most of the world's refugees and wealthier states in the Global North evade their responsibility by *paying* major refugee receiving states—in the form of cash payments but also economic aid and access to Western markets—to contain refugee populations abroad.[44] As indicated in chapter 1, while refugee resettlement in countries in the Global North has continued to receive the most public attention and praise, it is countries in the Global South that have consistently hosted the majority of the world's displaced refugees, often acting as buffer states that keep refugees from entering countries in Europe, the United States, Canada, or Australia.[45] In 2019, Global South states housed 85 percent of the world's refugees, while wealthier states in the Global North resettled less than one percent.[46] As such, the established international refugee regime, particularly the UNHCR, consistently prioritizes the sovereignty of states in the Global North at the expense of sovereignty in the Global South.[47]

In short, humanitarian aid is not merely about resolving refugee precarity; it is also bound up with a global governance that is designed principally to address the security and sovereignty concerns of Global North states.[48] This global governance is buttressed by humanitarian narratives that use the language of suffering rather than inequality, that invoke trauma rather than name violence, and that "mobilize compassion rather than justice."[49] To challenge the narratives of Western states rescuing and caring for the world's discarded, the next section reveals the hidden violence behind the humanitarian term "refuge," illuminating the role that these states played in inducing the "refugee crisis" in the first place.

The Refugee Paradox: The Problem Is the Solution

The crisis-rescue-gratitude story line disregards the fact that while nation-states denounce refugees as a problem, the precarious condition of "refugeeness" solidifies the importance of the nation-state and state protection.[50] The figure of the refugee, as a socio-legal object of knowledge, has been metaphorically central in the construction and promotion of Western state authorities. During the Cold War, refugeeness became a moral-political tactic, advancing the belief that the Soviet Union and nations of the Eastern Bloc were "illiberal and uncivilized" while assuring the allied Western nations that their respective form of governance was "civilized and moral."[51] In the United States, the propaganda value of accepting refugees fleeing communism—Eastern Europeans in the 1950s; Cubans in the 1960s; Southeast Asians in the late 1970s and 1980s—was central to the US foreign policy goal of broadcasting its brand of "freedom."

But the admission of refugees and other asylum seekers, touted as an act of humanitarianism, does more than boost the desirability and status of the Westphalian sovereign state. In the context of Western imperialism and globalized militarization, the centering of refugee rescue, bolstered by narratives of empathy and sentimentality, also deliberately *obscures* the "humanitarian violence" and racism of Western military empires.[52] In fact, as Didier Fassen reminds us, humanitarian language (and action) has become a dominant frame of reference for Western intervention and can be mobilized in military operations or in scenes of "natural disasters" in the form of epidemics and trauma.[53] In *Body Counts: The Vietnam War and Militarized Refuge(es),* Yến Lê Espiritu establishes that the figure of the Vietnamese refugee, the purported grateful beneficiary of the US gift of freedom, has been key to the (re)cuperation of American identities and the shoring up of US militarism in the post–Vietnam War era.[54] As she explains, Vietnamese refugees, whose war sufferings remain unmentionable and unmourned in most public US discussions of Việt Nam, have ironically become the featured evidence of the appropriateness of US actions in Việt Nam: that is, that the war, no matter the cost, was ultimately necessary, just, and successful. As such, it is the presence of the refugees—Việt Nam's runaways—that enables the United States to recast its aggressive military strategy in Việt Nam as a benevolent intervention. Indeed, the Jimmy Carter administration's massive Southeast Asian refugee resettlement program was devised in part to legitimize the United States as a leader in a new global humanitarian cause—and, simultaneously, to obscure its ongoing relationship with Prime Minister Pol Pot, who ruled over the mass killings in Cambodia in the late 1970s. According to Eric Tang, "For Carter, the figure of the refugee proved useful in answering the political quandaries of U.S. foreign policy."[55]

In short, refugee resettlement programs constitute a form of "geopolitical humanitarianism" that ends up affirming Western liberal democracies.[56] That is, humanitarian interventions are not merely about resolving a refugee problem; they are also practices that recuperate state sovereignty by eliding the fact that contemporary refugee crises are largely the result of the Western world's historical, sustained, and ongoing patterns of imperial and colonial violence and economic, social, and racial stratification. It follows that to make a case against these ongoing patterns of stratification, we need to reconceptualize the refugee not as an object of rescue but as a site of social and political critiques, whose emergence, when traced, makes visible the past, present, and future of Western imperialism and militarism that have been masked by humanitarian practices and pronouncements.[57]

Betwixt and Between: Refugees at the Nexus of Gratitude and Refusal

Re-storying: Refugee Stories/Refugee Lives

Stories. Refugee stories. Stories about and by refugees. Stories expose and shield; critique and restore; threaten and protect; violate and elevate; distill and instill; objectify and decolonize; hide and reveal. Stories ensconced in power; stories told on the run. Stories told in order to be granted asylum; stories told to speak back to power. Stories told to convey nothing; stories told to hold everything. Stories told to silence; stories told to obliterate silence. Stories born from war; stories born from beauty. Refugee stories; refugees re-storying. What is a story but a life?

Writing against the plethora of humanitarian texts by global humanitarians that reify condescending and depleted images of refugees, this section centers refugee authors and refugee stories that mix personal reflection with historical recollection and that revel in beauty and survival, even when refugee lives are edged with precarity. That is, it centers refugee *re-storying*. As Nayeri reminds us, "stories are everything": "In a refugee camp, . . . [o]ur stories were drumming with power. Other people's memories transported us out of our places of exile, to rich, vibrant lands, and to home."[58] Attentive to testimonies that "are seemingly not there," refugee authors ask readers to invest in refugee futurity and to manifest the reality that they wish to see. A powerful example: Ocean Vuong's novel, *On Earth We're Briefly Gorgeous,* is envisioned as a letter from a son to a refugee mother who cannot read. The narrator-son is thus writing not for the now but for the "not yet here." In the following excerpt, the son asks the mother to imagine a future in which she would find and read his letter.

> Ma, I don't know if you've made it this far in this letter—or if you've made it here at all. You always tell me it's too late for you to read, with your poor liver, your exhausted bones, that after everything you've been through, you'd just like to rest now. . . . I know you believe in reincarnation. I don't know if I do but I hope it's real. Because then maybe you'll come back here next time around. . . . Maybe then, in that life and in this future, you'll find this book and *you'll know what happened to us.* And *you'll remember me.* Maybe.[59]

The narrator hopes not only that the book will be found, "in that life and in this future," but also that wherever and whenever the book is found, the stories of "what happened to us" and who we were to each other will be there, waiting. The novel thus invites its (refugee) readers to look beyond the immediate present and to root themselves in futurity—not a humanitarian futurity that enfolds refugees into capitalist and heteropatriarchal desires, but a critical futurity that unfolds from refugees' everyday acts of resistance and affective forces in the here and now.[60]

In sum, the promise of refugee re-storying, of refugees writing for one another both within and beyond the time and space of refugee life, is this: once written, the stories—as a record, a witness, a testimony of refugee subject experiences—can lie in wait for future readers to find their way to them.[61] Refugee stories thus illuminate Walter Benjamin's conception of history and memory and José Esteban Muñoz's notion of queer futurity: the claim that there is no way to close off new understandings of the past and that it is precisely through the domain of storytelling—of the everyday in the here and now—that people remember, forge, and transform a past that is simultaneously suppressed yet based on "potentiality for another world."[62]

The Indebted: About Gratitude, Performativity, and Ambiguity

On the surface, the image of millions of displaced peoples from around the world, crossing treacherous seas by boat and jungles on foot and risking death in order to enter countries in the Global North, appears to affirm the latter's uncontested status as humanitarian nations of refuge. Yet, in *The Gangster We All Looking For,* the Vietnamese American writer lê thi diem thúy reminds us that not all refugees came running through the door that the United States allegedly opened: "There were things about us Mel [our sponsor] never knew or remembered. He didn't remember that we hadn't come running through the door he opened but, rather, had walked, keeping close together and moving very slowly, as people often do when they have no idea what they're walking towards or what they're walking from."[63] Like the characters in lê's novel, many refugees moved listlessly, with much confusion, indecision, and even misgivings, uncertain about what they were walking toward or what they were walking from. And a few even traveled away from the United States, such as the fifteen hundred Vietnamese refugees on Guam in 1975 who demanded to be repatriated to Việt Nam.[64]

In other words, the refugee flight-to-resettlement process is full of detours and snags, characterized "by chaos at the end of the war, confusion, and the stark absence of choice for many of those who had 'evacuated.'"[65] The messiness, contingency, and precarity of refugee life means that refugees, like all people, are beset with *ambiguity;* they—their stories, actions, and inactions— simultaneously affirm and trouble regimes of power.

Faced with "the stark absence of choice," refugees often possess little more than "their stories with which to fight for survival, rights, and wellbeing."[66] Nayeri explains how her refugee story defines her life trajectory: "In an asylum office in Italy . . . , we had to turn our ordeal [of fleeing Iran to escape religious persecution] into a good, persuasive story or risk being sent back. Then, after asylum was secured, we had to relive that story again and again, to earn our place, to calm casual skeptics."[67] In the following poem, the poet's expression of regrets for having "brought nothing" is followed by an offering of a story, the migrant's only possession.

Sorry
Sorry that we are here
. . . .
And sorry that we brought nothing
The only thing we have is a story
Not even a happy story.[68]

If, as the cultural studies scholar Mai-Linh Hong observes, "refugee stories are their currency," then the exclamation, "The only thing we have is a story," is decidedly ambiguous. As a medium of exchange for scarce goods and services (i.e., as currency), refugee stories can be genuine accounts of someone's life or concocted tales to obtain aid and protection—or both. The Rwanda-born writer Wamariya, who spent six years migrating through seven African countries as a child before being granted refugee status in the United States, disclosed that "one of the most valuable skills I'd learned while trying to survive as a refugee was reading what other people wanted me to do."[69] Karim Haidari, who escaped from Afghanistan to Germany, recalled that *lying* was his survival strategy. When asked for his passports and airline information by the power "behind the immigration desk," the English-speaking Haidari responded immediately with a lie: "No Anglish."[70] Many LGBTQIA+ refugees also have had to concoct lies to be believed. Ahmed Pouri, a Persian "refugee whisperer" who "has made it his life's work to teach refugees how to be believed by the Dutch," advised LGBTQIA+ asylum seekers to be "flamboyant" rather than nuanced: "Every gay person has to be a flamboyant scene-kid, out at clubs and fashion shows and on Grindr texting strangers at a night club. . . . [Y]ou have a better chance if you act out the cliché than if you try to convince them of a complex internal process."[71] Because what refugees conceive as their story will shape all their future days, Nayeri, Wamariya, and Haidari, and countless other vulnerable and exhausted asylum seekers, learn to tweak and tinker with their stories, injecting them with performative embellishments, silences, and lies—all in an effort to "refuse the political and economic hierarchies as the given of their destinies."[72]

As subjects of humanitarianism, hyper-aware of the need to perform vulnerability and gratitude, many refugees learn to fine-tune their life stories by enhancing or downplaying their experience, their joy or pain—in Wamariya's words, "to be who [they] needed to be and get what there was to get." In her memoir, Wamariya is piercing about the pressure to always appear appropriately grateful. With painstaking detail, she recounts the (in)famous 2006

Oprah episode on which her eighteen-year-old self (one of fifty winners of a national high school essay contest on genocide) and her older sister, in a quintessential made-for-TV Oprah surprise megamoment, were reunited on the show with their long-lost parents and siblings in Rwanda. As soon as Oprah triumphantly announced, after pausing for dramatic effect, " . . . your family . . . IS HERE!," Wamariya knew that she and her family had become characters in a "million-viewer spectacle [that was] being consumed by the masses."[73] Even as her sister "kept on her toughest, most skeptical face" and even as Waramiya felt a range of emotions—from joy and gratitude to relief to guilt—on the sudden appearance of her parents and siblings whom she had not seen for twelve years, her "refugee skills" took over and she "leapt up onto the set, smiling," performing with aplomb the expected role of Oprah's special genocide survivor.[74] Her "successful" *Oprah* appearance, where "everybody in the audience was crying," led to numerous other invitations. Waramiya became a sought-after spokesperson for genocide and in 2016 was appointed by President Barack Obama to the board of the US Holocaust Memorial Museum.[75]

Even when based in humanitarian language, these calculated performances of gratitude constitute rooted-in-lived-experience struggles that disrupt, however temporarily, the mythologies underlying humanitarian claims of refugee admission and resettlement. As such, refugees' "strategic performativity" is more than a defensive tactic that ensures survival and prosperity in a sponsorship-based economy; it is also a calculated action that exposes the uneven distribution of global resources as refugees maneuver to gain entry, shelter, and provisions—as they insist on their right to *more.* At the very least, it is important to acknowledge that refugees' strategic performativity is just that, strategic and performative, that refugees, who have minimal power and few resources, are self-aware as they playact the relationships and affects required of them to survive, and even to thrive.[76]

An example that encapsulates the tenet of refugees' strategic performativity is refugees' judicious deployment of the word *sorry*. In his novel *On Earth,* Vuong relays that *sorry* is the most common English word spoken in the Vietnamese nail salon where the narrator's mother worked. For the Vietnamese manicurists, *sorry* is not merely an apology; rather, it is a "tool one uses to pander until the word itself becomes currency"—a carefully orchestrated trade-in for a generous tip at the end of the manicure. Because "being *sorry* pays" and because "the mouth must eat," the definition of *sorry,* for Vietnamese manicurists, morphs into a new word entirely: "one that's charged and reused as both *power* and *defacement* at once." [77] Vuong's insights confirm that refugees' words, deeds, and intentions are often fluid and ambiguous, always tethered to material concerns. Conceptualizing refugees' performance of gratitude and deference as strategic rather than as misguided underscores the importance of grounding theory on refugees in concrete refugee struggles, attending always to the specific histories and contexts that shape their claims, that is, to the importance of narrowing "the gap that exists between existing analytics and emergent subject formations."[78]

Refugee Refusal: "The Ungrateful Refugee"

In 2018, twelve years after Wamariya's surprise reunion with her long-lost family on the *Oprah* show, during which she "was often cast as a martyr or saint[,] . . . so strong, so brave, a genocide princess," Wamariya decided to reclaim her personhood. In a

Washington Post interview on the publication of her memoir, *The Girl Who Smiled Beads,* Wamariya declared, "My name is Clementine. . . . I don't want to be called the genocide survivor anymore. No. It's a label. *I am human.*"[79] Likewise, in 2019, Nayeri, the Iranian American writer, tired of being pigeonholed for years as "rescued cargo," titled her first work of nonfiction *The Ungrateful Refugee,* in which she rails against "the compelling of gratitude toward the native-born. It is this feeling that immigrants get that they should go through their lives constantly bowing and showing their thanks to people who had very little to do with their rescue . . . , to show how lucky they feel."[80] In Berlin, Mohammed Jouni—Lebanon born, asylum seeker, high school student, founding member of an activist group of young refugees and asylum seekers in Germany—also insisted on refugee autonomy and humanity. As Jouni explained, when he spoke for himself rather than being spoken for by well-intentioned humanitarian advocates, "'the refugee becomes a person,' rather than an abstract idea."[81]

The above accounts—from Wamariya, Nayeri, and Jouni—constitute examples of *refugee refusal,* deliberate and willful moves to imagine and enact new subjectivities, new ways of being, and new freedoms that lie *just* outside the humanitarian refugee regime. In their groundbreaking work on the notion of refusal, Audra Simpson and Carole McGranahan contend that refusal, by definition, is a critique; it marks the point of limits having been reached. The act of refusing reframes, refocuses, and recenters the narrative and public discourse surrounding a given community; its intent is to "stop a story that is always being told."[82] For instance, Simpson's project on the nationhood and citizenship of the Kahnawà:ke Mohawks was motivated "by the complete disjuncture between what was written about my own people and the things that mattered the most to us."[83] Refusal is also an alternative to political recognition, a deliberate move away from accepting the legitimacy of state and other institutions to grant rights, recognition, protection, and social services. As both a political theoretical concept and a political practice, refusal signals a demand for alternative structures of politics that move "away from and in critical relationship to states."[84]

At the core, actors who engage in refusal understand themselves as subjects in opposition who *"refuse to continue on this way."*[85] For some refugees, this opposition arises from sheer exhaustion with managing the ongoing expectation of being *grateful*—a word that, according to Nayeri, comes up repeatedly and that hints and threatens and makes one afraid for the future.[86] To the rescuer, a gesture of gratefulness is free and should be readily bestowed; to the refugee, who is "tapped for gratitude by everyone [they] meet," it is "so costly"—to one's spirit, psyche, pride.[87] When the careful balancing of the costs to self tips too far to one side, when retellings of the "refugee story" become akin to pandering, when being a chameleon begins to feel the same as being a liar, refugees sometimes push back and move outward, simultaneously refusing and reclaiming the act of gratitude.

Nayeri writes, in *The Ungrateful Refugee,* that the problem is not that refugees are not grateful; rather, "gratitude is a fact of a refugee's inner life; it doesn't need to be compelled. Every day after rescue pulses with thanks."[88] As Vinh Nguyen explains, feelings of gratitude are not, or not only, sutured to liberal-democratic nationalism; given the innumerable losses suffered by refugees, they are also, or especially, expressions of genuine thanks for getting a second chance at life against the odds, "in situations where survival and success were not in the realm of expectation or even possibility."[89]

The problem is that for refugees, exhibiting gratitude is often the unspoken condition to acceptance, hospitality, and friendship, which removes their agency and dignity. Refusing the link between gratitude and "good refugee," Nayeri reclaims gratitude for herself: "My gratitude is personal and vast and it steers my every footfall. But it is *mine*. I no longer need to offer it as appeasement to citizens who had nothing to do with my rescue."[90] She further insists that admission of refugees by the United States is not extraordinary but "the obligation of every person born in a safer room to open the door when someone in danger knocks." As she exclaims, "It is your duty to answer us, even if we don't give you sugary success stories. Even if we remain a bunch of ordinary [Iranians], sometimes bitter or confused. Even if the country gets overcrowded and you have to give up your luxuries, and we set up ugly little lives around the corner, marring your view."[91]

But given how quickly overtures of hospitality to refugees can flip to displays of threats, refugee refusal, more often than not, materializes in a *roundabout* way—to protect refugees from the potential costs of exhibiting outright refusal. Wamariya's ambiguous response to intrusive questions about the Rwanda massacre provides a telling example. As discussed in chapter 4, media representation of refugees focuses relentlessly on the trauma and spectacle of atrocities and suffering, freeze-framing the "victims"—the dead, wounded, starving—in time and space, prolonging their decontextualized pain and agony in perpetuity. Such is the media coverage of the 1994 Rwanda genocide, in which some 800,000 people were killed in just one hundred days. In 2004, when the highly rated movie *Hotel Rwanda* came out, Wamariya was inundated with questions: Had anyone in her family been murdered? Had she seen people get killed? Inside, Wamariya seethed with anger: "I could not believe their sense of entitlement. These people did not have the right to my pain. . . . Their questions felt prurient, violating, evidence of their inability to see me as fully human."[92] Feeling like she was "disappearing, being consumed," Wamariya refused to become a spectacle: "I did not want to be a tool or a case study[,] . . . a curiosity, an emissary from suffering's far edge."[93] After declining numerous invitations to speak on her experiences during the war, she agreed to speak to a high school class, a school she would be attending the following year. Walking into the classroom, Wamariya knew that she did not want to share her interior life; so she simply didn't. Instead, she narrated her six years of migrating through seven African countries in search of safety "as an adventure. *I learned to speak seven languages. I wandered across a continent.*"[94] Wamariya sums up her refusal strategy: "I told a true story, though one that *conveyed nearly nothing.*"[95] The ability to tell a true story that conveys "nearly nothing" is yet another form of refugee re-storying; in this instance, it is telling *a* refugee story in a way that refuses *the* refugee story, one that is synonymous with violence, crisis, and disasters. This form of re-storying reiterates earlier ethnographic writings on violence that refuse to write, narrate, or interpret pain.[96]

In her examination of the historical cases from Indigenous North America and Australia, Simpson highlights the ways in which Indigenous people refused and still refuse to be folded into encompassing settler colonial narratives of acceptance.[97] In doing so, Simpson takes the notion of "refusal" to be an alternative to recognition politics in settler colonial society. Building on this insight, critical refugee studies scholars draw on refugee life to contest the assumed inevitability of refugee resettlement in the settler colonial host country. In a study of Cambodian refugees living in the Bronx in New York, Eric Tang shows how, in spite of the promise of redemptive US citizenship, the cycle of refugee displacement persists long after resettlement. The life conditions of Cambodian refugees in the Bronx—mired in poverty, street violence, deplorable housing, chronic unemployment—disprove the developmental narrative of the refugee as a subject of humanitarianism to be saved by liberalism, revealing instead the refugee as a subject of US imperialist warfare (in Southeast Asia) and ongoing divestment in late-capitalist urban America.[98]

Tang's study centers on the story of a single individual: Ra Pronh, a Cambodian refugee whose itinerant life included twelve different homes since her arrival in the Bronx in 1986. Refusing the liberal narrative of refugee transition and transfiguration, Pronh understood her movement from the Cambodian war zone to the Thai camps to the Bronx as "one long and unbroken state of captivity" and unsettledness.[99] When the 1996 Personal Responsibility and Work Opportunity Reconciliation Act ("welfare reform") was passed, Pronh considered negotiations with state officials futile since "the refugees never possessed anything with which to negotiate."[100] Drawing on her distinct form of refugee knowledge about the welfare state, Pronh knew she had to keep things moving herself by "hustling to find alternative sources of income and in-kind donations"—tactics learned while living in refugee camps and honed as a refugee in the Bronx.[101] Having survived the Khmer Rouge genocide, the civil war, the refugee camps, and nearly thirty years of Bronx unsettlement, Pronh refused to be bound to liberalism's empire of freedom. Opting for abstention from rather than engagement with the state, Pronh decided to jettison the state-based remedies proposed by others and the terms and claims of resettlement and to continue moving and hustling.[102] When refugees and asylum seekers bypass the state, like Prohn did, their refusal has the potential to forge a new kind of political space: "a possibility for doing things differently."[103]

Finally, in the post–Cold War era in which US imperialism and globalized militarization have taken the form of endless wars on terrorism, the displaced humans produced by these wars are cast as threats to be excluded and eradicated and not victims to be rescued and resettled. With the advent of the Trump presidency in 2016, anti-immigrant and antirefugee fervor has been mainstreamed; this fervor has persisted into the Biden presidency. During his presidency, Trump made barring refugees from the United States a priority; the Western world has also been plagued with a surge in nativism. As Eric Tang argues, "Today's refugees are construed as an entirely unique racial problem that reflects the public's anxieties over national security and is managed by practices such as racial profiling, surveillance, and detention rather than humanitarian resettlement."[104] Against the rise of nativist sentiment in the United States and in Europe, refugees and other irregular migrants have continued to insist that they deserve the same life options that are granted to native-born citizens. The sheer volume of "unauthorized" migration in the United States and in other countries in the Global North is a clear example of migrants refusing state regulations by going underground and forging new lives and social relations.[105] In the United States, the violent securitization of the US-Mexico border has not stopped migrant flows (see chapter 2). One contemporary example makes this point: according to Department of Homeland Security officials, in August 2020, even as emergency pandemic measures were established to rapidly "expel" most detainees, the number of migrants trying to enter the United States via the Mexico border continued to soar.[106] In the end, refugee refusal is refugees insisting that they must first meet their basic needs—whatever it takes.

Teaching Refugees/Refugee Teaching: A CRSC Initiative

As this chapter conveys, a key objective of critical refugee studies is to challenge the prevalent humanitarian narrative that turns refugees into dehistoricized objects of rescue and to feature instead stories that refract refugees through the lens of their humanity. At its core, this work is about flipping the script—from the *world's refugees* to the *refugees' world*. In this section, we provide an example of how the Critical Refugee Studies Collective has enacted this script by flipping not only in our scholarly writing but also in our organizing work on refugee education. Conceptualizing refugee students and their families as a source of knowledge rather than a problem to be solved, we insist on decolonizing the learning space by acknowledging, engaging, and elevating refugees' own experiences, knowledge, and creativity. That is, we flipped the script on refugee education by emphasizing *refugee teaching* rather than *teaching refugees.*

The United Nations Foundation, along with other humanitarian organizations, has consistently touted education as the key to brighter futures for refugee children: "Education is vital to children: It helps them learn skills, build confidence, and think critically. It also improves their chances at earning an income as adults and moving out of poverty."[107] In 2015, as world leaders gathered at the United Nations adopted the Sustainable Development Goals, which includes ensuring quality education for all children by 2030, the UN High Commissioner for Refugees, Filippo Grandi, pledged the agency's support: "Refugees face two journeys, one leading to hope, the other to despair. It is up to us to help them along the right path."[108] Grandi's pledge exemplifies both the promise and problem of humanitarian undertakings: the promise of needed resources, clout, and expertise and the problem of elevating the discursive frame of victimhood—"it is up to us to help them"—over refugees' own knowledge and initiative.

The UNHCR Teaching About Refugees webpage provides a telling example of this salvation narrative. Designed to assist "teachers [who] are facing new challenges in making sense of forced displacement and its complexities," the webpage provides teaching materials on refugees, asylum, migration, and statelessness and features a section "dedicated to professional development and guidance for primary and secondary school teachers in including refugee children in their classes."[109] Though well intentioned, the recommended teaching materials and assignments adhere largely to a model of Western sympathy and altruism that freezes refugee students and families in time and space, linking them perpetually to the past and to their place of origin—and to crisis and suffering. As an example, the "Including Refugees in Your Classroom" page features three main sections, all focusing on refugee students' perceived needs: "Effects of stress and trauma on children," "Successfully including children experiencing stress and trauma in your classroom," and "Understanding language acquisition." Cumulatively, the message is this: the teachers are there to rescue refugee children who are in need of care and tutelage.

On November 3–4, 2017, at the request of local teachers and refugee leaders, the CRSC hosted a two-day symposium in San Diego on refugee teaching,[110] with "refugee teaching" redefined to include teaching *by* refugees in collaboration with their families and communities. The symposium posed many of the same questions as other education events: How do school administrators, teachers, and counselors best support refugee students and their families? How do we build community with and for refugee students? How do we integrate refugee students into the school system? But, centering refugee knowledge, subjectivities, and lifeworlds, we added: How do we implement strategies for teaching that honor the unique experiences of refugee students? How do we design curricula that center refugee perspectives, refugee agency, and refugee epistemologies? How do we make refugee teaching social and affiliative, producing and reproducing community?[111]

Refugee parents and students were featured prominently in the symposium program. The symposium opened with a refugee parents panel, featuring four refugee mothers—two from Somalia, one from Congo, and one from Ethiopia—discussing (some through translators) their experiences with and expectations of the school system, as well as their hopes and dreams for their children. Perhaps emboldened by their position as paid speakers on a panel composed entirely of refugee mothers, they forcefully listed, citing specific examples of wrongs, what they wanted from their children's schools, at times appealing directly to the teachers in the room—with better teacher-parent communication topping the list. All four panelists also asserted that, irrespective of their English skills or familiarity with the US school system, they were attentive, invested, and capable parents, and they wanted to be treated as such. On the second day, all four students on the Refugee Students Panel emphasized that their perceived lack of English fluency often resulted in being steered away from advanced courses. One presentation stood out. In front of the packed auditorium, Samuel Sefu, a high school student who came to the United States from

Burundi just two years earlier, said to the audience, two hundred-plus strong, as he strode confidently across the stage: "I want to ask you a question: Do you think English equals intelligence?" Pausing just long enough for effect, Sefu slowly rolled out his answer: "Because I *don't!*" With a tinge of indignation, Sefu told his listeners, many of whom teach in the local schools, that his teachers often misrecognize his intelligence because of his perceived lack of English fluency. Sefu then informed the attentive audience that he and his family speak two languages—official Rundi (Kirundi) and French—and that other Burundians also speak a third language, Swahili, the language of trade.

In a context where refugee students and their families are often represented as a problem for teachers and school districts, Sefu's public refusal to accept the edict "English equals intelligence," along with other student panelists' insistence on access to a quality education, and parents' assertion of their rights to information all constitute examples of *refugee teaching*—that is, teaching done *by* and *for* refugees. Our next step is bringing schoolteachers together with refugee students and parents to collaborate on concrete lesson plans in history, literature, and science that center refugees' experiences and worldviews.[112]

Conclusion

Anchored in refugee epistemologies, experiences, and examples, this chapter is an emphatic critique of humanitarian-centered and rescue narratives that expect refugees to be forever thankful for the space they have been allowed. In Global North national spaces, resettled refugees perform the ideological work of upholding liberal ideals of freedom, democracy, and equality; they function as proof of the inclusive, tolerant, and fundamentally nonracist constitution of nation-states in the Global North.[113] And yet, through refugees' works and words, this chapter shows that true refuge is seldom found; and if found, it seldom fills. In the contexts of the hyperobjectification of refugees, displaced persons, and stateless human beings in the twenty-first century, as CRS scholars, we refuse, resist, and redirect idealized notions of restoration and resettlement, recognizing that hospitality is never forever, often comes with costs, and exists as a constant source of indignity for the recipient. It is not that refugees and other displaced human beings have not demanded more of the international refuge system; rather, the international system has not listened. Accordingly, it is humanitarians, not refugees, who need to adapt. As Nigel Hatton insists, humanitarians have to find "the words to speak to victims in the speech of the victims themselves"; and when they speak for the refugees, they need to find "the words that meet the humanity of victims and survivors."[114]

This chapter also elevates refugees' lived experience as a site of theory making, showing how refugee storytelling—refugee re-storying—allows for new forms of knowledge to be produced. In his work on Somali refugees, Mohamed Abumaye insists that "refugees are storytellers that engage in worldmaking practices through stories."[115] Refugees, as producers of knowledge, engage in the quotidian shared practice of storytelling as the vehicle through which to record and disseminate refugee knowledge about and against the humanitarian refugee regime. As displaced human beings rescued and/or shunned by global elites interested in object-stories for the sake of capital, recreation, and rescue, refugees reclaim their stories and objects and fill the universe and cosmopolitan plain with subject-stories that are imbued, organically, with life, dignity, and intersubjectivity.[116] As the writer Chimamanda Ngozi Adichie instructs us, "Stories matter. Many stories matter. Stories have been used to dispossess and to malign, but stories can also be used to empower and to humanize. Stories can break the dignity of a people, but stories can also repair that broken dignity."[117] Because, as Ocean Vuong reminds us, "we were [all] born from beauty."[118]

4   *A Refugee Critique of Representations*

On Criticality and Creativity

My sense of diasporic displacement and longing for my homeland [inform]
most of my art work. In relation to the Palestinian story, my art pieces raise
the visibility of Palestinian women within the art world. My sketches have a
narrative feature: the retelling of having witnessed these events. . . . The
viewer must study the body language and facial expressions in order to gain
insight into Palestinian women's subjectivity. My drawings are brought
together to tell a single larger story, the story of Palestinian women's
embodied trauma and resistance against the military occupation of Israel.

MARY HAZBOUN, quoted in LILA SHARIF, "The Permanent Sense
of the Diaspora in My Body"

The epigraph that opens this chapter is from the Palestinian artist
Mary Hazboun's own reading of her drawings in a series she calls
"The Art of Weeping." Heavily drawn in black against brown parch-
ment, the pieces in question are sketches of one-eyed women seemingly meshed together in rounded formations. Wound and bound
together, these figures look, on the one hand, malformed, as she
explains. On the other hand, they form a co-constitutive mass of
faces, veils, and arms, bodying forth a vital collective subjectivity

FIGURE 1. Mary Hazboun, *Women in War Zones*, 2019.

that is at the heart of the drawings (figure 1). Hazboun states that she draws from the lived realities of women and children; distilling these experiences into an embodied form, one that lives and breathes under occupation, she retells their stories of collective trauma *and* solidarity. She articulates how the forces of oppression and occupation create the form and content of her work, as they reshape the contours of the human body to critique the deforming effects of imperialism and militarism. Making visible the past and present displacement of Palestinians, Hazboun's work lends shape to the active ways in which the Critical Refugee Studies Collective theorizes refugees as agents of their own making, figures who are able to produce both culture and critique, both knowledge and narratives. Such ideas inspire and drive this chapter on refugee representations. Prompted by Hazboun's mode of drawing into being Palestinian subjects and the conditions of their "(un)livability" (see chapter 2), we ask: How does one read the cultural and artistic representations of and by refugees through a critical refugee studies lens?

To answer this question is to recognize that a CRS methodology takes refugees *at their word*. Similar to the critiques offered in previous chapters, wherein we take what is presumed in the discourses of the law and of humanitarianism and show their inherent limitations, a CRS mode of cultural analysis flips the script on commonplace understandings of refugees as they have been curated and mediated by the dominant culture. If earlier chapters made a case for needing a new lexicon for the enactment of refugee justice and care, this chapter urges us to find "new images" (to riff on NoViolet Bulawayo's book, *We Need New Names*) that depict refugee creativity and criticality. Here we provide a method of analysis that deconstructs—through a decolonial way of looking that uncovers colonial histories and roots out the asymmetrical power relations in colonialism—how refugees are often seen and yet not seen in media and culture.

This contradiction in the representation of refugees is explained most succinctly by Nevgat Soguk: "[Refugees] are visible even in their relative obscurity through representations that characterize them as disruptive externalities to host communities, posing political, economic, and security challenges. But as human beings, they are imperceptible and inaudible even when they speak, because of the condition of voicelessness imposed on them in formal and popular representations."[1] As Soguk suggests, while refugees are ironically both hypervisible and invisible, they are rendered speechless as well in the well-trod narratives of "trauma porn" in which they routinely appear in global media. Angela Naimou argues that the "doubled vision" of seeing and not seeing refugees perpetuates a "doubled violence" in the willful erasure of refugees' subjectivities. In European media, the labeling of refugees and their situation as a "crisis" only further obscures the context of political and economic violence from which they come. As Naimou writes,

"Whether reporters name it the 'European migrant crisis' or the 'European refugee crisis,' to invoke an ethics of hospitality or a politics of exclusion, the point here is that the crisis—the break and breakdown of order, the turning point, the time of decision—is denied its condition as legalized, chronic, and routinized violence inflicted on those already seeking refuge from violence."[2]

As in the US media, the language of "crisis" that often accompanies the word *refugee* demarcates a clear line between "us" and "them" and empowers the already powerful, those endowed with the ability to name the displaced as in/visible and voiceless/voiced in the Global North. The media theorists Noam Chomsky and Edward Herman have critiqued a contemporary mass media that is owned by a coterie of global media giants among which high levels of "concentrated wealth" circulates.[3] Robert McChesney also speaks of a "global communication oligopoly" in light of more recent media mergers and further deregulations within the industry.[4] At the same time that the media landscape is increasingly fractured and yet diversified with the advent of online and digital media, there is an intense competition, nonetheless, for the most clicks on stories and images in a single instance. Janet Wasko notes that "new communication and information systems, such as the Internet, are developing as a commercialized space" and that "this commercialization process—including the growth of advertising and public relations—has been accompanied by an ever-expanding consumer culture, thus prompting the term 'cultural capitalism' as a descriptor for the current period."[5]

Situated within the media currents of "cultural capitalism," it is often the case that with the refugee story, an emphasis on the sensational and spectacular is favored, an emphasis that forecloses analyses of the global historical conditions (of empire building, war, economic and political displacement, climate change) that produce the "crisis" and impel refugee movement in the first instance. Key to this apparatus is the reproduction of trauma porn and what remains "current" in the media, in which the "single story" is the currency of refugees and their symbolic capital.[6] This form of capital, in turn, produces the construction of another apparatus—that of Western governments, NGOs, and other groups that are characterized as progressive agents in the work to resettle and contain refugee movement. Thus under the sign of humanitarianism, or what Nigel Hatton has described as a "gift from the elite Western provider to the poor developing world recipient,"[7] and with an increasingly militarized presence, such agencies are produced and reproduced in the interlocking structures of power and capital that construct the paradigmatic refugee who is in dire need of saving.

Precisely because of this crisis in the representations of refugees, CRS gravitates instead toward art by refugees and, most resoundingly, to more private moments of grief, interiority, and reflection. This turn inward is what we pose throughout this book as a Feminist Refugee Epistemology methodology. These artworks often gesture toward less masculinist and nationalist public forms of expression as well as less salvationist narratives of rescue. We also centralize the work of refugees and their words to make the critical connections between their visions of justice and what Mai Linh Hong calls their "advocacy-art," which critiques the "nowness" of refugee conditions that often elides the *longue durée* of colonialism and militarism that precedes the moment of movement and flight. In contrast, advocacy-art, for Hong, is a mode of art making, whereby the "refugee's now is a strategic, dynamic now that dips into history when it must and recruits the future to implore the present."[8] We return to Hazboun's words to illustrate what we mean.

My artwork is a direct response to displacement. Displacement shaped who I am as a woman, and pushed me to grow and view life through a critical lens. I often always feel out of place, and when I go back and visit Palestine I feel out of place as well. I'd like to think of myself as living in between borderlands and that gives me a sense of freedom despite it being painful. I was able to reflect and cultivate my own views on life, culture, religion and the Palestinian struggle away from the mainstream nationalistic discourse and away from the cultural and religious institutions I grew up under. My Palestinian-ness pours into my displaced body; my displaced body lives on memory; my memory fuels my resistance; my resistance searches for the meaning of home through art.[9]

Hazboun's words craft a pointed and urgent narrative about colonial history but also of refugee refusal, refugee care, and refugee storytelling. She relates how time (as multifaceted and fluid) and space (as constrained and shifting) are expressed in the planes of her art and art practices and the vectors of her Palestinian identity as a diasporic female artist. Art making for Hazboun activates a mode of resistance in her work, which centralizes Palestinian histories of oppression and movements of liberation (figure 2).

As a form of knowledge production, Hazboun's drawings and retellings embody what Khatharya Um terms "refugitude,"[10] a temporal and spatial analytic that "connotes the state, conditions, and consciousness of being a refugee . . . [and] places refugee experiences and meaning-making at the analytic center, without dismissing the role of external forces and conditions in producing refugee dislocations."[11] Building on this concept, Vinh Nguyen speaks of "refugeetude" as a politically active mode of being that imagines justice in the future tense, often made manifest in acts of

FIGURE 2. Mary Hazboun, *Community*, 2019.

protest and cultural representations. For Nguyen, refugeetude also holds lines of relationality with theories related to decoloniality and affect. He writes, "Refugeetude . . . begins with but significantly departs from refugee—or a humanist move to redeem an abject position. Rather, it is to look at refugees anew, from a different angle, and ask how it can give rise to being and politics."[12]

Following Um and Nguyen, this chapter means to "look at refugees anew," leaning in to "listen closely"[13] to what refugees have to say—often with care and finesse—about how they author and create their narratives about being a refugee and more. We note that while narratives by refugees have been, in fact, diverse and expansive, spanning many regions and time periods, only a select few representations and their representatives are endorsed by cultural elites who circulate these texts within the Global North. Indeed, such is the problem of being "voiceless" that Viet Thanh Nguyen has described as the ways in which minoritized writers are chosen to speak in elite literary spaces.[14] We submit, however, that this mode of naming the voiceless and the marginal remains an old colonial tactic, as it denies our cultural worth as the creators of our own stories and producers of a knowledge that is worth knowing. Rather than accept this dynamic, we demand "true justice" in the ways that refugees are visualized and narrated in media and culture.[15]

In consonance with Hazboun's critiques of power, we demonstrate a cultural studies CRS methodology by exploring the tenets of FRE and discussing the ways that CRS scholars center refugee epistemologies and analyze gendered subjects in food, film, and art. We begin with a description of how refugee representations are usually conceived and received in the pages of global media and in art spaces in the Global North. Countering these sites and their representational politics, we discuss our efforts to promote refugee art (as that which has been created by refugees themselves) and to store and share refugee creations on our website, which we have named Refugee Archives, to showcase the art, writing, music, and media of and by refugees from any place in the world. Refugee Archives also serves as a digital site for the housing of refugee stories and histories. In the end, we advocate not only for the continual injection and flooding of refugee stories in all areas of cultural and political life but also for a careful mode of looking and listening that centers refugee agency and imagination. This, we posit, must serve as an antidote to the objectifying capture of refugees.

Consuming the Refugee: Art, Media, Technology

In April 2016, the Annenberg Space for Photography in Los Angeles, California, unveiled an art exhibition titled *Refugee*, which featured photography by well-known and award-winning photographers, a short film narrated by Cate Blanchett, and a virtual reality installation, all of which purported to document the lives and afterlives of refugees from Somalia to Syria, from Cameroon to Colombia. As the executive director of the Annenberg Foundation, Cinny Kennard, states in an interview with *Slate,* "While the topic may be overwhelming, this exhibition aims to illuminate the individual experiences of this population and put a human face on a staggering number."[16] Humanizing refugees, as we have argued previously, is predicated on the objectification of refugee pain and trauma. In the context of the Annenberg's *Refugee* exhibition, this is taken to another level altogether. On the night of the opening, befitting the glittering facade of the art space, young Hollywood actors like James Marsden, Amy Adams, and Rashida Jones arrived to fête the event, posing for cameras in front of life-size portraits of refugee men, women, and children and taking part in what critics have called the carnival of "celebrity humanitarianism."[17]

Precisely because of this sense of carnival, we doubt the exhibition coordinators would have expected that some attendees would also be refugees—people like us. When we visited the exhibition, it was a surreal and disquieting experience in the ways in which more than one hundred years ago W. E. B. Du Bois once described the feeling of "double consciousness": "this sense of always looking at one's self through the eyes of others, of measuring one's soul by the tape of a world that looks on in amused contempt and pity."[18] The exhibition encouraged a kind of looking that positioned the refugee subject-as-object and was manifested in its built environment as well as in its high-tech interior. The following analysis does not attempt to evaluate the aesthetics of the work in the exhibition itself but rather interrogates the political economy of this space and what the accumulation of art objects in it says about how the Global North often sees and apprehends refugees, a gaze that is complicated by the fact that "we" identify with/as the refugees in question.

Before entering the exhibition space, we were confronted with the hyper-capitalist surroundings in which it is embedded. The Annenberg Space for Photography stands among a phalanx of parking lots (where a security guard checked the trunk of our cars) and towering commercial buildings that make up the business district of Century City in Los Angeles. The building is nestled between the Century Plaza Towers, which were designed by the renowned architect Minoru Yamasaki. These two towers, phallic in shape at forty-four stories, are supposed to mirror the Twin Towers in New York City, and as with its predecessors, the Century Plaza Towers serve as the epicenter of commercial activity in the area. Most notably, they house office spaces for the Hollywood elite, including agents and lawyers, and the brokers of finance and global capitalism. The art space is a built environment, constituted by a cool and sleek complex of curved spaces and technologically enhanced rooms that encase the visitor in the visual imagery of refugee precarity. That refugees are now the cause célèbre for organizations like the Annenberg Foundation speaks to the ways that the refugee figure can be highly aestheticized and used as a form of currency for the power brokers of culture and celebrity.

One of the images featured at the exhibition was of Alan Kurdi, the two-year-old Syrian boy of Kurdish ethnic descent who was found dead on a beach in the Bodrum Peninsula in Turkey. Kurdi, his brother, Ghalib (four years old at the time), and his mother, Rehanna, all drowned after their overloaded boat had capsized. Photographed by Nilüfer Demir, this image first appeared on September 2, 2015, on the front pages of many global media outlets, sparking outrage and concern about the plight of Syrian refugees. Its heavy circulation among these outlets was "estimated to have appeared on 20 million screens in the 12 hours since the discovery of Kurdi's body, . . . included in 53,000 tweets, on the social-media platform Twitter, every hour."[19] The simplicity of the photograph lends itself to this kind of reiterative traction, for in minimalist detail, the image of a toddler dressed plainly in blue shorts and a red shirt speaks as a metonym for the tragedy of mass global displacement. As a metonym, according to the news editor Dimitri Beck, it communicates an "essential truth" about refugee suffering in its excision of other details surrounding the picture,[20] for example, the Italian patrol officer who was also on the scene and Ghalib's and Rehanna's deaths at the same time; these aspects of the drowning cannot visually and viscerally compete with the close-up of Kurdi's inert body on the shore. What results is, in the end, a beautiful image, and, as Emily Regan Willis argues, it is all the more horrific because of it.[21]

This photograph, among the other large portraits of refugees at the exhibition, was surprisingly small in size in comparison, but the symbolism of Kurdi's photograph was momentous, signaling how refugee suffering is often represented in bodily terms. In the impulse to "humanize" refugees through a visual rhetoric that objectifies the refugee body, refugees become iconic symbols of victimhood. Imaged as broken bodies that elicit calls for "our" humanitarian assistance, these bodies are gendered feminine and rendered childlike in many instances, naturalized as such in the media's imagining of refugees as abject and without rights.[22]

While it is supposedly a taboo to publish and circulate images of dead children, as Willis reminds us, "not all dead are treated the same,"[23] to which one can add that, therefore, not all responses to these images are the same. As such, pictures of dead children are published and circulated widely, evoking a form of identification and a paternalistic need to protect on the part of those consuming such imagery. As Kurdi was a small, light-skinned child, wearing a simple red shirt and blue shorts, he could also stand in for a universalized child subject, whereby the infantilized refugee is defenseless and needy (see chapter 3) but this time through a colorist and colonial lens. As Peter Bouckaert of Human Rights Watch observes, Kurdi's photograph confirms the implicit biases in this form of identification when he notes that the pictures of African children who were found dead on the shores of Libya, published a few weeks before Kurdi's, did not have the same impact on the global audience as Kurdi's image did.[24]

Refugees are not only racialized in the media; they are also gendered in their rendering. Media images of male migrant bodies, who represent the threatening countenance of terrorism and radicalism in the post-9/11 era, carry a volatile charge, one that becomes tempered by the representation of urgency and masculine distress. Featured in the *New York Times* in 2015, for example, the Pulitzer-winning photographs by Tyler Hicks, Sergey Ponomarev, and Daniel Etter show male refugees who are part of the fleeing, terrified masses. Several of these photojournalists' images are mostly of men who collectively struggle against the tides of the ocean, hold onto one another, and cry for their loved ones, in ways that dramatize the plight of refugees and evoke biblical connotations of exile and exodus. Fittingly, our response to refugee imagery is often one of concern, but it is ultimately salvationist in nature. The ways in which these images articulate the theme of rescue and redemption are not coincidental. As Terence Wright argues, the image of the paradigmatic refugee that dominates in Western media is anchored to Western art and Christian iconology. He writes, "Many of the pictures that we see of refugees conform to pre-established patterns. For example, in Christian religious painting we find a long tradition in portraying forced migration which can be traced from 'The Expulsion from the Garden of Eden' to 'The Flight into Egypt'; such images have played a central role in the development of Western visual representation."[25] Beautifully shot and highly aestheticized, the *New York Times* photographs remind those in the Global North of our (Christian) obligation to rescue and save. Above all, the imagery of refugee emergency works as a synecdoche to elicit the impulse to act quickly and without haste to aid the "suffering." As Pooja Rangan argues in relation to recent documentary practices that purport to humanize the voiceless in film, the rendering of suffering as immediate and concerning (what she calls "immediation") is highly problematic, as it "privileges action over thinking, ethics over aesthetics, and immediacy over analysis."[26]

The concern for refugees' well-being is also founded in the representation of an epic struggle between life and death itself, wherein refugee humanity is only identified when it hinges on suffering; their "bare lives," to use Giorgio Agamben's words,[27] are exposed as the symbolic currency that refugee media imagery relies on for its commodification and circulation. As Prem Kumar Rajaram notes, the image of the refugee, as someone displaced from the protective confines of territories and the "speechlessness" ascribed to them, "conditions forms of therapeutic state-centric responses," whereby "through the processes of repatriation or resettlement, the refugee is introduced into the family of nations."[28] The refugee's muteness only amplifies the requirement that an agency or expert speak for them, thus "reinforcing the state-centric political imagination; refugees become a site where certain forms of knowledge are reproduced and justified. What the refugee is left is biological corporeality."[29] Lisa Malkki argues that the reduction of the refugee to the mute image of the body is the condition upon which a dehistoricization of the refugee subject is enacted and a "universal humanity" asserted.[30]

Undergirding this imagery of universal humanity and mute victimization is a concept of the human family as a universal and heteronormative construct in and of itself. Refugees are rendered even more "incapacitated," as they are pictured to be struggling to live and survive without the visual signs of familial ties and support,[31] which then call out for state forms of assistance that would intervene and care for them. Implicit in these state structures is a heteronormative logic that values how the refugee subject is monogamous, cisgendered, and desirous of family relations and reunifications, a subject who is essentially a "good citizen." "Same-sex migration policy organizes sexuality," as Audrey Yue argues about Australia's immigration laws, "around the heteronormative institutions of intimacy and the family, incorporating the queer migrant as a good citizen through self-cultivation and disciplinary regulation."[32] By the same token, state care and protection can also be homonationalist in many Global North contexts. Particularly acute in the post-9/11 context, the Western state, for example, champions LGBTQIA+ rights by granting asylum to queer migrants often from Muslim countries but in accordance to binaristic notions of gender and sexuality.[33] Showing proof of the persecution of their sexual minority status creates a double bind for refugees, one that adheres to Western constructs of being "out" in a context of visibility.[34] In privileging LGBTQIA+ liberties, the Western nations look to themselves as bastions of secularist liberalism, while other countries remain illiberal and backward as it relates to gender and sexual rights and religion. According to Jasbir Puar, these "highly contingent forms of nationalism" acquire their "greatest purchase through comparative transnational frames rather than debates within domestic realms."[35] The move to portray other countries in this way, as Eithne Luibhéid contends, works to "reinforc[e] the self-congratulatory posture inherent in the geopolitics of asylum" while erasing the fact that the Global South is actually host to a majority of the world's refugees and asylum seekers (see chapter 3).[36]

In either image or text form, the broad appeal often made on behalf of the abandoned and the "orphaned" is based on damage and endangerment, the language of which is encoded in the 1951 UN Convention Related to the Status of Refugees (see chapter 1), and must always foreground injury and trauma. As a consequence, this damage-based approach requires the performative gesture for migrants to embody a kind of persecuted suffering and familial abandonment that would show proof of bodily and/or psychic injury. Exploring the limits of this rhetoric, the literary scholar Lindsay Stonebridge insists that the politics of a "horrified humanitarianism," which undergirds the response to images like Kurdi's, has always been severely deficient in addressing a durable and ethical program of care for refugees.[37]

The optics of how refugees "look" or are "looked at" matter in the circulation and consumption of refugee imagery that makes a plea on behalf of the refugee subject, a kind of supplication that sustains the power relations between those looking and those who are looked at.

These practices of looking must be examined closely for the kind of colonial gaze and imperial logics that they engender. Cropped from such snapshots, and, indeed, absent from the space of the art exhibition in Los Angeles, are the frames of war, imperialism, and militarization that structure the conditions of global displacement—and our complicity with such processes. Displaced from view are the invisible relations of power that broker how we see and consume the refugee subject. While refugees are ubiquitous in mainstream culture and media, they signal very little beyond the fact of their suffering. As the literary critic Sladja Blazan puts it, "The omnipresence of refugees on television, computer and tablet screens, and in daily newspapers, theaters and literary works is striking. At the same time, refugees are only seldom represented or even understood as agents."[38]

Mounted on the walls of the Annenberg Foundation, the photographs similarly focused on refugees and their lack of agency, a leitmotif that was bolstered by the exhibition's use of state-of-the-art technology. Within an eye-shaped room, for example, a film about refugees and the photographers who photograph them ran on a continuous loop; surrounded by wall-to-wall sound and images, you can watch the film in its panoramic display from either side of the room and feel engulfed by the many images of refugee deprivation. In a virtual reality (VR) installation, you can immerse yourself in refugees' experiences by looking through a virtual headset; each cubicle (four total) allows you to interact three-dimensionally with and view the home environs of one of the refugees, who hail from four different countries. In the women's bathroom, you can observe a short film done via hologram images that demonstrates how the VR display was made. By way of virtuoso technology, then, you are invited to witness and participate in the simulated worlds the globally displaced inhabit. In the process, the ways in which military technologies, including but not exclusive to virtual reality, the geographic information system (GIS), and the global positioning system (GPS), also used to surveil and police communities of color today, were normalized in our everyday forms of looking in ways that "mobilize us as consumers of militarization."[39] As these examples show, the exhibition works hard to dissolve the boundaries between the viewer and what is being viewed, between the spectator and the spectacle, for "you" are ostensibly present with "them" in experiencing how they live in their destitution. Shaped by twenty-first-century technologies, the exhibition reasserts a colonial way of viewing refugees as childlike and needful, a way of viewing that is guided by both a consumptive gaze and an omniscient eye.

Feminist Refugee Epistemologies, Critical Juxtaposing, and the Intimacies of Hearth and Home

The severely burned Phan Thị Kim Phúc, screaming, arms flailing, running naked down a Vietnamese road after a napalm attack in 1972; the lifeless body of the drowned toddler Alan Kurdi, lying facedown on a Turkish beach in 2015—these powerful iconic images, focusing relentlessly on the trauma and spectacle of war atrocities, freeze the "victims" in time and space, prolonging their pain and agony in perpetuity. Intended to shock, visual images of "Third World" suffering in Western media—of the dead, wounded, starving—constitute generic decontextualized horrors that elicit pity and sympathy, not discernment and assessment. As Rey Chow has argued, Americans have increasingly come to "know" the world as a target.[40] When wars break out, foreign areas and peoples briefly enter US mainstream public discourses, often via deeply disturbing images of suffering, as embodiments of (naturalized) violence, crisis, and disasters.[41]

In the preceding section, we discussed refugee imagery in art and media, wherein the hyper-focus on suffering and the outpouring of outrage and concern over dead and injured refugees substitutes for a need for serious analysis of the geopolitical conditions that produced their displacement in the first instance. Constructed for Western consumption, these spectacular(ized) images are also masculinist, rendering invisible and inaudible the everyday and out-of-sight struggles as well as triumphs of the displaced as they manage war's impact on their lives.[42]

Writing on Vietnamese and Syrian women artists and the politics of the everyday, Yến Lê Espiritu and Lan Duong lay out the contours of a Feminist Refugee Epistemology when they posit a deep study of artists and their art practices to examine how they reclaim the private sphere as a gendered space expressive of both creativity and loss.[43] With respect to this inner domain, the authors ask: If these spectacular acts of military atrocities are the markers of violence, then what offscreen violent acts remain unmarked? What are the affected spaces that exist behind, between, and beyond these public(ized) spaces? If access to home and security comes under the purview of the masculinist state and policy makers, then what questions about place and belonging remain unaddressed? What are the desires—and not only the needs—of the forcibly displaced, as they create improvised, fluid, and alternative homemaking, healing, and survival strategies on the run? In short, how do we approach the question of gendered displacement from the knowledge point of the forcibly displaced, which takes seriously the hidden and overt injuries but also the joy and survival practices that play out in the domain of the everyday?

Centering the more mundane, routine, and open-ended dimensions of war and displacement, FRE reconceptualizes time and space not as natural and fixed but as materially and discursively produced—*and* unsettled and remade—by refugees. In so doing, FRE treats the forcibly displaced not as objects of analysis but as sites of knowledge production, contributing to the emergence of critical theory *from* the Global South. We press for notions of refugee *life*, not only in terms of their livelihood, which once again emphasizes the refugees' victimhood, but also and especially about their lived lives—how they have created their worlds and made meaning for themselves. In the Indigenous scholar Eve Tuck's eloquent words, "Even when communities are broken and conquered, they are so much more than that—so much more that this incomplete story is an act of aggression."[44] Most of all, this approach incorporates the material, ethical-political, and creative dimensions of knowledge production and presses on the importance of feminist collaborations in the formation of ideas and arguments, collaborations that advance a reflexive reading of power and privilege.

For a dynamic engagement with refugee lifeworlds, Espiritu and Duong turn to the Syrian visual artist Nisrine Boukhari, whose work addresses questions of nomadism and belonging and of coping with the loss of one's city. They contextualize her art against the family's history and exilic condition, her art education in Syria, and the Syrian War and the displacements that she has continued to experience. In their historically situated cultural analysis, the authors take note of the present everydayness of Boukhari's sense of exile, since she lives outside of Syria and cannot return home.

Aspects of Boukhari's past and present thus crisscross the grain of her work. Away from Damascus, Boukhari notes in an online interview that she experiences a deep loneliness: "When we leave

FIGURE 3. Nisrine Boukhari, *Unreceived Letters*, 2014, installation. An ongoing project since 2012 in different cities in the world.

our city or country, we carry these places within us. When I left Damascus, I felt that I lost something bigger than the loss of a person. It was harder than breaking up with a lover. I felt this loss badly when I moved without having the will to move."[45] To connect herself to Damascus, Boukhari takes to writing quick daily notes, in the form of unsigned letters addressed to the city that she left behind, about what was in her mind about the state of exile, the conditions in Syria, and the city that she lived in, among other concerns. As she explains, "These small notes let me feel that I am still in relation with my place while I am living my loneliness out of it."[46] Such text fragments, which reposition her in relation to her former home, form the content of *Unreceived Letters*, an installation about a personal case study of a city—Damascus—from the perspective of exile (figure 3). The setting is simple: the letters are placed in an open wooden box, which is set on the floor surrounded by doilies, on which viewers are invited to literally sit with the letters—reading, touching, thinking, reminiscing with them. While these letters certainly allude to the violent conditions in Syria, they do not rely on suffering feminized bodies to do so. Rather, Boukhari's words and artwork testify to the power of thinking through and speaking aloud the interiority of loss and grief.

Pivotal to this reimagining of the refugee and the place of interiority is the home. For CRS authors, one of the critical affordances of Feminist Refugee Epistemologies is that it enables a resiting of the home as a place for the housing of feminist, queer, and trans solidarities and socialities, markedly away from the masculinist and nationalist sphere of the public. While underscoring a throughline of a decolonial feminist critique in our writings, our scholarship also offers instruction in the ways that a CRS method of analyses can be deployed to interrogate a range of cultural productions that includes literature, art, film, and food making. Food, its mode of production and consumption, its connections to colonialism and empire, has been especially generative as a node of inquiry for scholars looking at refugee cultural productions and the ways that refugee food can be understood as a transnational commodity within the global marketplace. As the editors of *Eating Asian America* make clear, a study on Asian American gastronomy reveals "the cross-articulation of ethnic, racial, class, and gender concerns with the transnational and global circulation of peoples, technologies, and ideas through food, cooking, and eating."[47]

Linking these analytical nodes with a critical refugee studies methodology and emphasizing ethnographic history from a Feminist Refugee Epistemology perspective, Lila Sharif connects Palestinian women and the making of food to a wide swath of alternative histories, memories, and knowledges that remain and reside in the home. In her work, Sharif brings together refugee studies and FRE with food studies, arguing that food becomes a productive site in which Palestinian women make sense of and negotiate the ongoing condition of settler colonialism. Sharif posits that "memory" is not a passive depository of events passed but an active process of creating meanings that are liberated from the hegemonic constraints of fixed notions of history. The inheritance of memory from homeland to diaspora resonates in Sharif's mode of ethnography and the self-reflections that permeate her writing. In the case of Palestinian women and their presence within the kitchen, memory allows for the resuscitation and transmission of subaltern subjectivities, particularly when they are assumed to have been "vanished."[48] Sharif's CRS methodology is to engage directly with Palestinian women, taking them at their word but also delving into a study of their speech and bodily performance. Sharif looks closely and listens attentively to her subjects' narratives to posit that Palestinian women reconstitute food sites into places of cultural transgression; in this reconfiguration, the home is where Palestinian women have historically resisted Israeli power as well as cultivated, celebrated, and memorialized the land and the fact of their living.

As part of the Palestinian diaspora herself, Sharif observes a moment of "colonial unknowing" by the end of her essay: although she has intimate knowledge of her subjects and their histories, she realizes her interviews resist her own claims of the women's "vanishment." She writes, "What has become particularly evident to me during my conversations with Palestinian women is the ways in which settler-colonialism is never complete because of Palestinian insistence on life. In a sense, I am writing against myself—against the vanishment I have theorized—by instead going to Palestinian kitchens and groves where I have been reassured by Palestinian women, that everything is not lost—that life remains even when things are rapidly and tragically falling away."[49] An important aspect of CRS analyses is the self-reflexivity and self-reflection that we, as refugee scholars, often express in our research. In so doing, we reject the falsehood that academic writing must be objective and our perspective impersonal, as the themes of displacement and the acts of community making—of collaboration— are living and breathing subjects for us in the work we do within the academy and beyond it.

Similar to Sharif's focus on the home as a site for a FRE inquiry, Lan Duong's reading of the short film *Nước* (2016) by Quyên Nguyen-Le interprets the final scene as emblematic of the making of queer feminist subjectivities in the home.[50] *Nước* explores the maternal lineages that connect trauma and restoration, delving into the realms of Vietnamese refugee grief and loss, as well as maternal nourishment and abundance. With its narrative setting of everyday places, for example, early on we are placed inside a dark room where we first discover the protagonist's mode of processing war memory or a beauty salon where the mother, a Vietnamese refugee, retains the bruise of a memory she has of the war in Việt Nam. These everyday spaces and intimate places provide a recognition and establishing of what Ly Thuy Nguyen calls a "queer dis/ inheritance" and "refugee future." Nguyen delineates how a "refugee future, as such, is not ensured through capitalist success story or an inherited bloodline, but rather by enacting a sensory connection patched with, for example, favorite memories of mother's special homemade food for rare occasions, passed down as an invitation to include her children's queerness. In the final scene,

FIGURE 4. Rosie being pulled to shore by Mẹ. Quyên Nguyen-Le, *Nước*, 2018.

[then,] we reenter this conversation to witness Mother telling her queer child to 'invite your friend next time I make porridge,' a gesture that we can read as latent recognition and acceptance of a queer lineage."[51]

With its focus on the unspectacular nature of refugee acts of love and survival, the mother and genderqueer child (Rosie) eat their food communally against a US cultural context that Nguyen-Le demonstrates only operates to fetishize the Vietnam War and dehumanizes Vietnamese women (at one point, the song "Me So Horny" is played in the background of Rosie's scene of self-birthing). Moreover, creative power underlies the intimate spaces cited in *Nước,* but it is the primal relationship between mother and child that constitutes the film's main affective artery. In the penultimate scene, the protagonist pulls out from their uterus a bloody umbilical cord. In a scene of painful gestation and labor, they work to get the cord out, but with the same kind of pulling gesture, we then see the mother pulling Rosie out of water onto a boat, in effect saving their life and steering them toward safety (figure 4). As this scene makes clear, water's lifegiving powers are vested precisely in a conflation of mother and country, woman and family.

In exploring the expansive refugee lifeworlds that Vietnamese diasporic filmmakers like Nguyen-Le create on the screen, Duong's analysis foregrounds the meanings rooted in the texture of words, visuals, and sounds in film. Intimate acts of food making and eating signify "worldmaking" practices that are addressed specifically to Vietnamese queer and trans subjects in the diaspora. We come away knowing that Rosie's mother makes their home more hospitable for her queer child, thereby resisting the heteropatriarchal injunction to eject LGBTQIA+ children or kin from the home. Moreover, Nguyen-Le's film embodies what Long Bui calls the "refugee repertoire," that which is "a reconstruction of postmemory [that] draws on stories, texts, and images to innovatively understand war trauma and apprehend the particularity of being children of refugees. . . . The performative repertoire of refugees narrativizes disjointed lives and subjectivities not only to question history and memory but also to communicate the adopted poetic forms of play and pleasure forged by dispossessed youth imprinted with the violence of their communities on their bodies."[52] In the context of *Nước,* making the home more habitable and mitigating the violent imprint of the war on Rosie's body is a part of the refugee repertoire that Bui speaks of (figure 5). But even more resolutely, the feminist act of home-making opens a space for queer refugee lives and desires to find refuge inside the home. In short, Duong is concerned with a CRS examination of culture that is anchored in refugees and their "complex personhood[s]"[53] and that pays attention to the rich and complicated lives that refugees lead.

FIGURE 5. Rosie eating cháo. Quyên Nguyen-Le, *Nước*, 2018.

An engaged form of ethnographic practice, a deep textual analysis, historically informed contextualizations of the conditions from which artists create, and collaborative modes of thinking and writing: these are the CRS methods of analysis that are foundational to our scholarship and vision of collective liberation. It goes without saying that creative works by refugees deserve our scholarly time, energy, and attention but also a methodology that takes into account the artists' agentive take on refugee history and memory. The discussion that follows illustrates this point even more emphatically in describing how the CRS Collective has facilitated the making of refugee art and refugee archives on our website.

Refugee Art/Refugee Archives

Countering the impulse to "humanize" refugees, either in art spaces like the Annenberg Space for Photography or on the pages of global corporate media, critical refugee studies insists that these misguided efforts to humanize refugees rely on their dehumanization and strip them of the ability to narrate their own lived realities and experiences. Pivoting away from such spectacles, we focus instead on what the Foundland Collective (made up of the artists Lauren Alexander and Ghalia Elsrakbi, who are based in Cairo and Amsterdam) has called the "small stories" of refugee displacements. These small stories are rooted in a desire to "slow down what we are seeing in order to focus on details related to the situation and connect this to larger and other historical narratives."[54]

The concept of small stories underlies the ways in which CRS scholars think and write, as we turn away from the media's trauma porn and decenter the power relations in the ways in which we "look at" refugee subjects. Therefore, we do not take for granted the distinction between "us" and "them" with respect to our privileged position in theorizing about refugees. The word *we* is repeatedly used in this primer to underscore the importance of collectivity—of collaborations in the formation of ideas and arguments, collaborations that, we believe, must always advance a reflexive reading of power and privilege.

Beyond our published writings, we are committed to decoupling the idea that "who we are" is separate from "what we do" in other sites, namely, through our website (www.criticalrefugeestudies.com). In addition to organizing conferences and collaborating on book projects, the CRS website represents a form of cultural labor that pronounces the importance of refugee enactments in terms of stories and histories, of art and the archive. Debuting in 2017, the website concretizes the kinds of interventions, communities, and conversations we want to create with one another and others in both actual and online spaces. With the goal of being informative and interactive, it extends our dialogues with activists, academics, and artists from around the world. Scattered across multiple tabs and webpages, criticalrefugeestudies.com presents as an aesthetic object itself, featuring on its banners and backdrops beautiful artworks by transnational artists like Lin+Lam, Sokuntevy Oeur, Gina Osterloh, Lang Ea, Kou Vang, and Tiffany Chung. On what we see as a virtual canvas are our theories put into practice, or to use Cherríe Moraga and Glorida Anzaldúa's words, "theories made into flesh,"[55] about how the figure of the refugee is a social actor, one who has always imagined other worlds, other possibilities, through creative expression.

Our approach to grant giving also makes space for the multiplicity of refugee livability as we uplift the works of not only academics, but also students, community organizations, and artists whose works range from advocacy and community building to film, music, and art (see chapter 2). Not only do we promote refugee art through our website, but we have also financially supported artistic projects by both individuals and community organizations. From 2016 to 2020, with funding from the University of California Office of the President (UCOP), we provided undergraduates, graduate students and junior faculty and nonprofit organizations with funds for research and community-oriented projects that innovatively focus on refugee communities, memories, histories, and experiences. But equally important, we offer grants to cultural workers who want to develop and actualize their art projects and need the (seed) money to do so. Consequently, our grants have helped to facilitate a rich archive of music, literature, films, artwork, and performance that spans a range of genres, themes, and aesthetic expressions. Our artist grantees are also strikingly diverse; they originate from and form the diasporas of such countries as Iran, Ethiopia, Venezuela, El Salvador, Somalia, Laos,

Cambodia, and Việt Nam, among many others. Most often the people we fund find funding in the arts a very difficult endeavor; they sometimes lack access to locating such grants and funding sources or are sidelined because their work is understood to be too ethnic identified, marginal, and/or community oriented. It has been key for us to identify these groups to financially support and highlight their contributions to the making of art, the realms of which are elitist and exclusionary. With these grant-giving activities, our mission is to celebrate the creative acts of refugees as profoundly agentive and imaginative.

Along with this mission, we recognize the need for refugees to create their own stories, but we also identify the need for a space for us to share and redistribute them. Refugee Archives serves as a repository to house refugee creative expression. This part of the website provides digital storage space for the uploading of "artifacts" that delve into refugee lives; as such, users from anywhere in the world are able to upload artifacts that are their own artwork, stories, images, music, and videos. Any genre of art, literature, music, film/video, and performance can be published by the artists themselves. Users can also manage these items once they are up, adding to, deleting, and editing their work as they see fit. We hold no ownership to the works; we simply create a digital space so that they may be stored and accessed virtually.

In designing the Refugee Archives and delineating its purpose, we overturn what an archive usually denotes. Usually, archives denote a physical space, one that is supported by institutions and organizations and made accessible to an interested and often privileged public. With their collection of artifacts, ephemera, and documents, the archives' holdings are understood to contain the historical record of a group, community, society, or nation. The contents not only tell about the past but also serve as an authoritative repository for the documents and storied deeds of heroes, inventors, leaders, and so on. The theorist Jacques Derrida argues that while the institutional archive is very often focused on the past, it also anticipates the future and future publics in that it foretells how it should be used by the state, the individual, and the public.[56] Precisely because of these issues of power and history striating the archive, the Haitian scholar Michel Trouillot contends that the act of archiving is itself an act of power, one that works to revivify the power of those in the archive and to silence those who are absent from it.[57]

Drawing on the archive's power, we conjoin "refugee" with "archives" to privilege that which is powerfully underwritten and managed by refugee artists themselves. Our archives are not only about refugees; they are made by refugees. Refugee Archives operates as both a description of what the archives are, with "refugees" serving as an adjective, and what refugees are empowered to "do," that is, archive our own stories—an important move because, as the poet and theorist Yousif Qasmiyeh puts it, "the refugee has never assigned herself the role of the initiator of the archive."[58] The CRSC founder Ma Vang argues that as a concept, the refugee archive is potent in capturing what she calls a Hmong "history on the run." She writes that the refugee archive is a "key method with which to emphasize the embodied and material aspects of histories that run and the spiritual dimension of forced displacement without recovering the loss."[59] As profoundly, at another crucial level, Refugee Archives allows us a space where we can speak to one another in the language of aural, visual, and written poetry and record and preserve the joys, sorrows, memories, and desires that border our lived realities. In addition, it has always been imperative for us to decenter the notion of an institutionalized archive and its attendant preoccupations with access and privilege with a virtual space that is open, interactive, and bears witness to our creative and critical being.

Conclusion

This chapter discusses the material and digital means by which the Critical Refugee Studies Collective strives to theorize refugee lifeworlds and put these ideas into a method and praxis. The website and its function speak to our imperative for interactivity and creativity; that is, since its establishment in 2018, we have continually asked that users interact with it by contributing to our archives as well as our blogs and story maps. At heart, our efforts are directed toward constructing the communities with whom we want to be in a conversation. If this chapter began with Mary Hazboun's words describing the community of Palestinian women who inspire her art and politics, we end with a larger call for more stories and the formation of more communities. Underlying this request is an invitation to make possible and material the public with whom we mean to create transformative change. Such are the beginnings and borders of what we want to fashion—that is, "new critical communities"—as one way to work toward social justice for the globally displaced.

Conclusion

In/Verse

walking with ghosts
        mending
    wading through
            wake work
messiness of life
   "love to the point of not being able to forgive . . . "
               what could have been
     stories that get waylaid
    the body remembers
her hands have been instrumental to her survival
     never trust a map
circles rather than lines
        potentialities of the in-between spaces
filling empty spaces
              holding space
journey
      pleasure
practice as research
     meditation, yoga, rap, poetry, storyteller
     dehumanization is constantly flipped by communities of color
         survival and beyond
     peace builders

genuine gift

joy

We inspire . . .

REFUGEE VOICES culled from presentations at the "Secrets and Stories" CRSC conference, Merced, California, November 15-16, 2019

In ending with a larger call for more stories and the formation of more communities, we are not simply demanding "more" for the sake of accumulating and collecting stories and making them speak ethnographically. Let us be clear: we are asking for those plentiful stories that would constitute an arsenal to decolonize and wrest power from the powerful. And with these stories, we mean to query, as Christina Sharpe has so lovingly etched into her writing, "what beauty as a method might mean or do: what it might break open, rupture, make possible and impossible. How might we carry beauty's knowledge with us and make new worlds."[1] Building on Sharpe's questioning, we propose new communities that would constitute these "new worlds" that she calls into being.

What would these new worlds look like? It would begin in/ verse. The poetic words above, articulated, without coordination, by various refugee community members, scholars, and students throughout our days-long conference, emphasize the ways that we view refugee acts in verse and in acts of storytelling. We string these phrases together in poetic form to speak aloud their poetic content and impact. Spontaneously spoken and gathered, they are placed in this book's conclusion as an antidote to the bloody or bloodless terminologies that structure how we often talk when we talk about refugees. This book began with the profundity that refugee stories carry, and we end similarly, reiterating the depth and meaning of what we see as poetry in refugee words, particularly in the snippets of conversation and dialogue we have (over)heard at our conferences. The reliance on poetry here relates to the structuring logic for the book; reading poetry as praxis, we have understood the work and acts of refugees as a poesis that has the power to invert dominant narratives. And as an inverse of conventional modes of reading and listening, this book tenders more, more stories and better modes of apprehension as they undergird and relay the refugee's expansive worlds.

In imagining these new worlds, refugees summon us to create innovative methods of analysis and form new critical communities. The literary scholar Mary Layoun has urged that we listen to and look closely at refugee self-representations, which include oral histories and testimonials, as well as fiction and nonfiction literatures. For they relay more than just narratives of damage; such works open a space for critics and readers to distrust and critique hegemonic narratives of power. At the same time, they hold an enormous charge for the creation of new communities that would receive, distribute, and read them. Layoun writes that in refugee narratives lie "an incisive critical edge . . . , a persuasive argument for a calculated (mis)trust in dominant narratives, a skeptical recounting of failed critical communities, [and] an urgent appeal for new critical communities."[2]

We make an urgent appeal for the formation of new critical communities in collective spaces. At the Critical Refugee Studies conferences, we hold spaces that are essentially *community* spaces where refugees can take refuge from an outside gaze that seeks to invisibilize them. The folks who have participated in our conferences have been visitors, interested faculty, and students and community members, as well as our grantees who have helped us imagine what is possible in the building of the field of Critical

Refugee Studies. Our conferences, which have taken place over the years at the University of California, San Diego, Los Angeles, Merced, and Berkeley, are sites where in the pre-COVID era we communed over words, theories, images, music, poetry, and food. Each of these conferences has created community spaces that bring the university into the fold and not vice versa.

Or, as Alexis Pauline Gumbs has queried powerfully in critiquing the university and its necropolitics toward People of Color, "Did Audre Lorde and June Jordan teach in prisons, coffee shops, living rooms and subways so that I could pretend that the university has all the real classrooms and everything else must be a side hustle?"[3] The "side hustle" for us is made central in the space of the CRSC conference, a structure of feeling in community that we aspire to continue with every project we see to fruition. Similar to our website's request to form a community that would remake the world, our conferences facilitate the bringing together of communities that strive for collective liberation and social justice for the globally displaced. Moreover, justice for "just us" is embedded in a transformative justice paradigm integrally related to abolition work.[4] The activist and writer Mia Mingus's definition of these two terms—"transformative justice" and "abolition"—is key as it illuminates on how these terms are separate but inherently related. Mingus states:

> Abolition is the ending of prisons, the prison industrial complex, and a culture of prisons (e.g. criminalization, punishment, disposability, revenge). Transformative justice is a way to respond to violence within our communities in ways that 1) don't create more harm and violence and 2) actively work to cultivate the very things that we know will prevent violence, such as accountability, healing, trust, connection, safety.

I understand abolition to be a necessary part of transformative justice because prisons, and the PIC [prison industrial complex], are major sites of individual and collective violence, abuse, and trauma. However, transformative justice is and must also be a critical part of abolition work because we will need to build alternatives to how we respond to harm, violence, and abuse. Just because we shut down prisons, does not mean that these will stop. Transformative justice has roots in abolition work and is an abolitionist framework, but goes beyond abolishing prisons (and slavery) and asks us to end—and transform the conditions that perpetuate— generational cycles of violence such as rape, sexual assault, child abuse, child sexual abuse, domestic violence, intimate partner abuse, war, genocide, poverty, human trafficking, police brutality, murder, stalking, sexual harassment, all systems of oppression, dangerous societal norms, and trauma.[5]

We demand transformative justice and abolition for our communities in the wake of so many changes that have been wrought in 2020 and 2021 and beyond. This book concludes with a robust appeal for "new worlds" and "new critical communities," premised on the enduring hope for better things that are yet to come. We reiterate that refugees are not only social actors and critics but also storytellers. Our emphasis on storytelling asserts that to be a narrator of one's experiences, family histories, and community formations is to be vested with courage and imagination. We ask you to reconceive the ways that refugee stories and histories are deeply shaped by both a creative and a critical impulse. And in so doing, we invite you to create a new critical community with us, which together we—as part of the ungrateful and rageful refugee masses— are rightfully due.

Epilogue
A Letter to UNHCR

August 25, 2021

Dear United Nations High Commissioner for Human Rights;
Cao ủy Liên Hợp Quốc về người tị nạn;
Gudida Sare Qoxootiga Aduunka ee Qaramada Midoobay;
Chère Haut Commissariat des Nations unies pour les réfugiés;
Liebe Hoher Flüchtlingskommissar der Vereinten Nationen:

On the recent celebration of your seventieth anniversary
(December 2020) and in anticipation of your seventy-fifth (December 2025), we, the Critical Refugee Studies Collective, want to
invite you to join us, or for you to invite us to join you, in rethinking
UNHCR definitions, approaches, and knowing of refugees. We
speak not only as a collective of scholar-artist-activist-family
members; we carry messages provided to us by refugees who
demand more from the UNHCR: they want us to tell you to train
your employees to treat refugees with respect and dignity, they
want us to tell you to support grassroots organizations and the
knowledge they can provide to guide UNHCR practices, they want
us to tell you to take their meetings, to offer consultations, to
present more opportunities for you to listen to them.

Importantly, we want to firm up your understanding of the refugee story, give it the heft, respect, dignity, and rigor you direct toward presidents, nations, the law, international relations, governance, sovereignty, complementarity. True, the refugee story is elusive, creative, and perhaps available to more human beings in ways more than other forms of expression, discourse, and knowledge. You do not need to go to story school or hire a storyteller in the same way you might need law school or legal representation. But we contend that you should take as much care with a person's story as you do with their legal case, their medical records, their personal information, or any data that the law requires you to respect, protect, and only share when in the best interest, agency, and permission of the person.

In the German language the word for refugee is *fluchtlinge,* taken from *fluchten,* which means to flee. *Fluchtig,* in German, means volatile. Thus, in German, UNHCR is the UN Agency for People Who Flee. The person who flees as the refugee is similar in many other European languages, particularly in the progressive North. With flight and volatility forever marked on refugee identity, it is difficult to tell their true stories. Unknowingly or unwittingly, you have abused story and its natal relationship to the arts to render refugees as the fleeing masses, the 84 million people who are the problem of our time. We are troubled by the *sad* stories you continue to circulate around the globe—on your website, in brochures, at award-winning photography exhibits, in professional television commercials, and through star-studded Hollywood celebrity speaking campaigns. These stories are striking, colorful, enchanting even, and baring barely a blemish as you attempt to show blemishes in our humanity and call for increased donorship, awareness, and care for refugees, displaced and stateless persons, and asylum seekers, to a segment of the world busy with capital gains, leisure, parties, promotions, and selfies by the sea at the perfect angle in the perfect light.

We understand and hold some amount of sympathy for your method, your motivations, and your fight for meaning and persuasion in transnational thinkspaces saturated with more messages, appeals, demands, and campaigns than reasonable human beings can be asked to process in the course of their daily lives. To rise above the informational mass, you have decided, a famous actor, a beautiful actress, a well-known athlete, European, European American, wealthy, comfortable, and of progressive mind, can garner support otherwise denied. Celebrity, as an antidote to indifference, you seem to suggest, begets identification and concern, the privileged seeing the unprivileged, and in turn, donations that enable a professional humanitarian class the resources, incentives, benefits packages, pay, and other means to act and to save and to rescue refugee lives. For this reason, your graphic designer's vision and your photographer's camera lens must be as strong and precise as possible, capable of zooming in on broken limbs, tears, sandals, despair, children in mothers' arms, intricate knits and fabrics of ethnic wardrobes and head wraps, and indicators of loss and nothingness (mud, bellies, boats, random t-shirts with commercial logos, etc.). We get it: as you see your mandate and pathway to success, helping refugees requires that we spectacularly see their suffering. As early as Voltaire and Rousseau, certainly even before, this method has guided Western European and U.S. American hands, thinking, and penmanship toward the other—it has been directed toward efforts to humanize (sic) pagans, slaves, women, and now refugees, in the eyes of intolerant or uncaring societies. Sad stories, then, for the UNHCR in the twenty-first century are a type of global currency, a catchy way to generate some quick cash and cache.

There has to be—and is—a better way.

One of your recent stories begins with the sentence, "Grandmother Magdalena recalls the despair she felt when she fled Venezuela at age 60." The next sentence starts with the word, "Escaping . . ." In a matter of two sentences, a woman, who we later learn taught law school at university, is rendered a South American grandmother-figure, an escapee, one who flees, one who despairs. Her law school education, her university position, her equality, and credentials are subjugated to the tropes and narrative of an old woman in the Global South fleeing, rescued, and grateful to the West for her evacuation and safety. How has Grandmother Magdalena's law background helped the UNHCR? In what ways has Grandmother Magdalena spoken the law into her relationship with the UNHCR? Have any staff been trained with Grandmother Magdalena? How have Grandmother Magdalena's intellectual contributions informed UNHCR policy? We will never know if the formula of refugee identity remains escape, despair, and rescue.

While Grandmother Magdalena is a law professor, we realize that not all refugees have the privilege of education or professions prior to their separation with their home countries. Oftentimes, the unequal conditions they face at home or that led to the experience of their need to leave result from imbalance, violence, and theft projected onto them by Western democracies. Yet, all refugees, whether professors, doctors, dancers, farmworkers, or homemakers, produce knowledge, knowledge of value to UNHCR and other agencies, knowledge embedded in their stories that we have asked you to handle with a greater level of care and seriousness. This request we make of you is not inconsistent with the demands of the High Commissioner for Refugees Filippo Grandi, who told a group (the Third Committee of the UN General Assembly) in 2020 "that refugees, like migrants and others on the move in this era of extraordinary human mobility, are not just vulnerable people in need of help—they are also strong, effective, courageous contributors to communities hosting them, and to societies as a whole. We have seen it in hospitals, in old people's homes, in supermarkets, in businesses and community organizations—on the many frontlines of this unprecedented global struggle. This is important, as it counters the toxic and unproductive narrative depicting them as a threat and a burden."

We have addressed this letter to you to emphasize our belief that you need to improve your relationship to story; refugee campaigns need to come from a genuine place that has refugee agency, thinking, dignity, and respect at the center. Keep the lens caps on your cameras, furlough your graphic designers, retrain your communications division and workforce, rethink your employment ads, Nobel Prize-striving, and find new ways to envision maps, charts, statistics, photographs, envelopes, laws, policies, that better value and emphasize refugee knowledge.

We have addressed you in the form of a letter to constitute the power of address, the dignity of an exchange between the you and the we, the you and the I. We also think of the innumerable appeals refugees have written to the UNHCR, the letters found on refugees as they tried to make it to safety, the letters refugees have sent and send to loved ones, unread letters, letters written to the Critical Refugee Studies Collective about the UNHCR, and the letters that begin with the words, Dear UNHCR. This book and the books in the Critical Refugee Studies Collective book series are parts of arts and letters that expand on the issues we raise with you here. Read these texts for more detailed information, more exacting concerns, and more analyses of problems. They offer humane, scientific, rigorous, creative, scholarly, and grassroots ideas on how to avoid "toxic and unproductive narrative depicting (refugees) as threat and a burden" and how to prepare UNHCR staff to avoid these dangerous tropes.

We see you, applaud your work, acknowledge your powerful position in the world when it comes to helping refugees. Answer us. Write to us because there has to be—and is—a better way.

Signed,

The Critical Refugee Studies Collective

Notes

Prologue: A Letter to Our Communities

1. UNHCR 2020b.
2. Nguyen 2016.
3. See Kestler-D'Amours 2021.
4. In 2020, we also endured one of the most polarizing presidential elections in US history.
5. Covid Data Tracker 2021.
6. See Oppel et al. 2020.
7. See Akee 2020.
8. See McFarling 2020.
9. Fueled in part by Trump's use of racially charged terms like "Chinese virus" and "Kung flu," racially motivated harassment and assaults against Asian Americans have skyrocketed during the pandemic, including a wave of attacks against elderly Asian Americans in the early months of 2021. See Tang 2021.
10. Barboza and Poston 2020.
11. Welna 2020. Note that this death toll tally of 58,220 American dead discounts the number of the 3 million war dead in Việt Nam, including 30,000 Hmong soldiers and 50,000 to 150,000 Cambodians.
12. Day 2020, 1.
13. Buchanan, Bui, and Patel 2020.
14. Buchanan, Bui, and Patel 2020.
15. Poujoulat 2020.

16. Quoted in Güner 2019, 1.

17. Pirtle 2020, 504.

18. Pirtle 2020, 504.

19. Beech and Hubbard 2020.

20. Vang 2021, 8.

21. Vang and Myers 2021, 3.

22. Volpp 2015, 292.

23. Volpp 2015, 292.

24. Neal 2020.

25. Tang 2015, 14.

26. Butler 2006, 15.

27. Hamdi 2011, 40.

28. See our website, www.criticalrefugeestudies.com.

29. Cafferty and Clausen 1998, 96.

30. Roy 2020, 13.

31. Roy 2020, 13.

Introduction: Departures

1. Lorde 1984, 110.

2. Said 1990, 362. For further definitions of refugee and related terms, see also the official United States Citizenship and Immigration Services discourse at www.uscis.gov/humanitarian/refugees-and-asylum/refugees and at the "Definitions" section of the Immigration and Nationality Act (INA) (8 USC 1101) especially 1101 (a) (42) for the definition of "refugee" (https://uscode.house .gov/view.xhtml?req=granuleid%3AUSC-prelim-title8-section1101&num= 0&edition=prelim):

> (42) The term "refugee" means (A) any person who is outside any country of such person's nationality or, in the case of a person having no nationality, is outside any country in which such person last habitually resided, and who is unable or unwilling to return to, and is unable or unwilling to avail himself or herself of the protection of, that country because of persecution or a well-founded fear of persecution on account of race, religion, nationality, membership in a particular social group, or political opinion, or (B) in such special circumstances as the President after appropriate consultation

(as defined in section 1157(e) of this title) may specify, any person who is within the country of such person's nationality or, in the case of a person having no nationality, within the country in which such person is habitually residing, and who is persecuted or who has a well-founded fear of persecution on account of race, religion, nationality, membership in a particular social group, or political opinion. The term "refugee" does not include any person who ordered, incited, assisted, or otherwise participated in the persecution of any person on account of race, religion, nationality, membership in a particular social group, or political opinion. For purposes of determinations under this chapter, a person who has been forced to abort a pregnancy or to undergo involuntary sterilization, or who has been persecuted for failure or refusal to undergo such a procedure or for other resistance to a coercive population control program, shall be deemed to have been persecuted on account of political opinion, and a person who has a well-founded fear that he or she will be forced to undergo such a procedure or subject to persecution for such failure, refusal, or resistance shall be deemed to have a well-founded fear of persecution on account of political opinion" (1101(a)(42)).

3. Mignolo 2009.

4. Emerging work in CRS includes Ma Vang's *History on the Run: Secrecy, Fugitivity, and Hmong Refuge Epistemologies* (2021), and Mohamed Abumaye's "Askar: Militarism, Policing, and Somali Refugees" (2017), which is forthcoming in print.

5. While the spectacle of chain-link cages in ICE detention centers has been a prominent example, this development also includes the preemptive family splitting that refugees practice prior to and during migration, such as the sending of unaccompanied child migrants from Central America. See Casavantes Bradford 2019b.

6. Bacon 2000.

7. Um 2015, 16.

8. Vuong 2019; "Ocean Vuong" 2019.

9. Karell 2002, xxxiii.

10. Lorde 1980, 12.

11. Ong 2003, 47.

12. Baldwin 1992.

13. Boonmee Yang's poem, "the reason we indent," appears in *MAI*, a community zine edited by See Xiong (Yang 2017, 6). Xiong received a Critical Refugee Studies Collective grant in 2017 to support her work on *MAI*, whose purpose is "to share community stories by Southeast Asian Americans about their experiences in Southeast Asian America." See https://criticalRefugeestudies.com /grants/2017-grant-awardees.

1 A Refugee Critique of the Law: On "Fear and Persecution"

1. Ogata 1951, 4.

2. Ogata 1951, 4.

3. UNHCR 2011.

4. Hong 2020a, 36.

5. UNHCR 2011.

6. Um 2015.

7. www.unhcr.org/en-us/climate-change-and-disasters.html.

8. www.unhcr.org/en-us/climate-change-and-disasters.html.

9. UNHCR 2018, 2.

10. UNHCR 2018, 2.

11. Jayawardhan 2017, 105, 115.

12. UNHCR 2002.

13. UNHCR 2002.

14. UNHCR Asylum Lawyers Project 2016, www.unhcr.org/en-us /5822266c4.pdf, accessed December 8, 2020.

15. UNHCR Asylum Lawyers Project.

16. White 2014, 980.

17. Koçak 2020, 31.

18. White 2014, 989.

19. White 2014, 983.

20. UNHCR 2019.

21. UNHCR n.d.c.

22. UNHCR Global Trends 2018. www.unhcr.org/globaltrends2018/.

23. US State Department, https://2009–2017.state.gov/j/prm/policyissues /issues/protracted/index.htm.

24. "The Future of Refugee Welcome in the United States," International Rescue Committee Report," 2017, www.rescue.org.

25. UNHCR Global Trends 2018.

26. Musarat-Akram 1999, 215.

27. For example, Lebanon hosts 173 refugees per 1,000 of its population. See UNHCR 2017.

28. Hyndman 2000.

29. Hyndman 2000, 2.

30. Hyndman 2000, 2.

31. UN, OAU Convention: Governing the Specific Aspects of Refugee Problems in Africa, 1969, www.unhcr.org/en-us/.

32. UNHCR 1984.

33. Casavantes Bradford 2019a, 45.

34. Casavantes Bradford 2019a, 43, 46.

35. Villagran, Connolly, and Montes 2019.

36. Dickerson 2020.

37. Nowrasteh 2020.

38. Pew Research Center 2021.

39. Cheatham 2019.

40. Casavantes Bradford 2019b.

41. "Family Separation under the Trump Administration—a Timeline," 2020.

42. Kopan 2018.

43. Congressional Research Service 2019.

44. Flagg and Calderon 2020..

45. Casavantes Bradford 2019b.

46. Casavantes Bradford 2018.

47. Cohn, Passel, and Gonzalez-Barrera 2017.

48. The executive order halted all refugee admissions for 120 days and banned Syrian refugees indefinitely. It also temporarily barred people from seven Muslim-majority countries (Iran, Iraq, Syria, Yemen, Somalia, Sudan, and Libya) from entering the United States.

49. Vang 2021, 143.

50. Soguk 2007, 283–308.

51. Stack 2020.

1. For a critical analysis of how Pacific Islanders seek to resist environmental degradation such as coral reef destruction to restore balance through climate justice, see Quintanilla 2020.

2. Swain 1995, 5.

3. Ogata 1951, 4; emphasis added.

4. Soguk 2007, 192.

5. www.aclu-nj.org/theissues/immigrantrights/waronterrorismislikewaroni.

6. Wood 2004.

7. Soguk 2007, 292.

8. In 2021, worldwide there were around 470,000 refugees and asylum seekers from El Salvador, Guatemala, and Honduras—a figure that registered an increase of 33 percent as compared to 2018. www.unhcr.org/en-us/displacement-in-central-america.html. See also https://rosanjose.iom.int/SITE/en/blog/migrant-caravans-explained.

9. Aguilar 2017, 78–79.

10. Smith 2018. Reprinted on the Poetry Foundation website.

11. Hong 2020a, 34.

12. Hong 2020a, 37; original emphasis.

13. Stevenson 2014, 14.

14. Stevenson 2014, 18.

15. See Vo Dang 2005.

16. White 2014, 990.

17. See De Genova 2010b.

18. White 2014, 990.

19. White 2014, 992.

20. Hope 2019.

21. Cheatham 2019.

22. Dickerson 2020.

23. Casavantes Bradford 2019b.

24. Paik 2020, 103.

25. Dickerson 2020.

26. Feldman 2018, 138.

27. Gregory 2004, 78–79.

28. Rempel 2000.

29. Akram 2014, 2.

30. Rempel 2000.

31. Euro-Mediterranean Human Rights Monitor 2021.

32. The website of Rafeef Ziadah, www.rafeefziadah.net/.

33. See Erakat 2019.

34. Qutami and Zahzah 2020, 75.

35. On the exclusion of Palestinians from the 1951 Convention Relating to the Status of Refugees, see Akram 2014, 2.

36. Critical Refugee Studies Collective website: https://criticalrefugeestudies.com/resources/critical-vocabularies. See chapter 2 for further analysis of this definition.

37. Critical Vocabularies on the Critical Refugee Studies Collective website: https://criticalrefugeestudies.com/resources/critical-vocabularies.

38. See https://criticalrefugeestudies.com/resources/critical-vocabularies.

39. "Empire," Critical Refugee Studies Collective Website, https://criticalrefugeestudies.com/resources/critical-vocabularies.

3   A Refugee Critique of Humanitarianism: On Ungratefulness and Refusal

The epigraph from Dina Nayeri is found in The World Staff, "This New Book Confronts 'Good Immigrant' Stereotypes, Rethinks Gratitude," *The World*, September 4, 2019, https://theworld.org/stories/2019-09-04/new-book-confronts-good-immigrant-stereotypes-rethinks-gratitude. Accessed November 1, 2021.

1. Lipman 2020, 8.

2. Hyndman 2000; Rajaram 2002.

3. Nayeri 2017.

4. Hong 2017.

5. Nayeri 2017; emphasis added.

6. Blazan and Hatton 2016, 98.

7. Klaas 2016, 194.

8. Wamariya 2019, 2.

9. Wamariya 2019, 2.

10. Wamariya 2019, 1.

11. Wamariya 2019. 4–5.

12. Oh 2012, 34.

13. Klaas 2016, 193.

14. Klaas 2016, 199.

15. Klaas 2016, 194.

16. Klaas 2016, 194.

17. Casavantes Bradford 2019a, 16–17.

18. Klaas 2016, 204.

19. Nguyen, 2012.

20. Barnett 2002, 251.

21. Fassin 2012, x, 7.

22. Hatton 2016, 127.

23. Hatton 2016, 127.

24. Muller 2013, 470.

25. Hyndman 2000, xxii.

26. Hatton 2016, 126. In a speech to the UN Assembly, UN High Commissioner for Refugees, Filippo Grandi, acknowledged the tremendous knowledge production of refugees, but the seamless incorporation of that knowledge production into global institutions and their philosophies and personnel, remains aspirational: "Two weeks ago, at the opening session of this year's UNHCR Protection Dialogues, I held a discussion with a group of young women and men, all refugees or activists, who have distinguished themselves through exceptional contributions to fellow refugees and host communities, helping them respond to the coronavirus pandemic in different, creative and effective ways—as doctors, community workers, information providers, and mobilisers. It was an exceptionally inspiring debate—their energy, determination and enthusiasm matching their smart insights on what needs to be done to support, heal, include, and unite. What I learned in that debate—the thoughts it provoked—is what I would like to leave you today as my main message. It is a reminder that refugees, like migrants and others on the move in this era of extraordinary human mobility, are not just vulnerable people in need of help—they are also strong, effective, courageous contributors to communities hosting them, and to societies as a whole" (Grandi 2020).

27. Hatton 2016, 126.

28. Ong 2003, 52–53.

29. Ong 2003, 64.

30. In recognition of their work with refugees, the Nobel Peace Prize Committee awarded the UNHCR the Nobel Peace Prize in 1954 and in 1991.

31. Fassin 2012, x.

32. Hyndman 2000, xvi.

33. Ong 2003, 146.

34. Barnett 1995; Mertus 1998, 331–334. Academics, policy makers, and journalists also participated in the construction of these refugee "crises" as the products of sectarian conflicts. See Jasser 2014; Peteet 2010; Leenders 2010; Nebehay 2014.

35. Mertus 1998, 339; Hyndman 2000, xix.

36. Hyndman 2000, 5.

37. Hyndman 2000, 187.

38. https://www.unhcr.org/en-ie/5b698cb97.pdf.

39. European Civil Protection and Humanitarian Aid Operations 2020.

40. Barnett 2002, 254–55.

41. Barnett 2002, 262.

42. Espiritu 2014; Barnett 2002; Abumaye 2017.

43. Barnett 2002, 262.

44. Fee and Arar 2018.

45. Espiritu and Ruanto-Ramirez 2020; Arar 2018.

46. UNHCR 2019; Fee and Arar 2019.

47. A key example: Jordan, a major refugee-hosting nation that houses 2.7 million refugees in a total population of 9.5 million, often has to rely on international humanitarian institutions like UNHCR to broker and provide emergency relief to house, feed, and provide social services to refugees. See Arar 2018.

48. Barnett 2002; Soguk 2007.

49. Fassin 2012, 7.

50. Soguk 1999, 16.

51. Lippert 1999, 305.

52. Atanasoski 2013.

53. Fassen 2012, 158.

54. Espiritu 2014.

55. Tang 2015, 36.

56. Liu 2002, 9.

57. Espiritu 2014.

58. Nayeri 2019, 6.

59. Vuong 2019, 240; emphasis added.

60. See Jones 2013.

61. Muñoz 2009.

62. Benjamin 1973; Muñoz 2009, 1.

63. lê thi diem thúy 2003, 8.

64. Lipman 2012.

65. Lipman 2012, 5.

66. Hong 2017.

67. Nayeri 2019, 8.

68. Cited in Soguk 2007, 294.

69. Wamariya 2019, 5.

70. Haidari 2002.

71. Nayeri 2019, 232, 237.

72. Soguk 1999, 306.

73. Wamariya 2019, 7.

74. Wamariya 2019, 5; see also Krug 2018.

75. Wamariya 2019, 7; see also Krug 2018.

76. Bui 2016.

77. Vuong 2019, 91-92; emphasis added.

78. McNevin 2013, 199.

79. Krug 2018; emphasis added.

80. The World Staff 2019.

81. Quoted in McNevin 2013, 196.

82. Simpson 2014, 177; Simpson 2017; McGranahan 2016.

83. Simpson 2007, 72.

84. Simpson 2014, 19.

85. McGranahan 2016, 320; original emphasis.

86. Nayeri 2017.

87. Nayeri 2019, 116.

88. Nayeri 2019, 344.

89. Nguyen 2013, 344.

90. Nayeri 2019, 344; emphasis added.

91. Nayeri 2017.

92. Wamariya 2019, 106.

93. Wamariya, 2019, 108, 107.

94. Wamariya 2019, 107; original emphasis.

95. Wamariya 2019, 107; emphasis added.

96. McGranahan 2016; Das 2006; Visweswaran 1994.

97. Simpson 2017.

98. Tang 2015.

99. Tang 2015, 15.

100. Tang 2015, 94.

101. Tang 2015, 92.

102. Tang 2015, 170.

103. Simpson 2014, 29.

104. Tang 2015, 176.

105. De Genova 2010a, 39.

106. Miroff 2020.

107. United Nations Foundation, https://unfoundation.org/blog/post/5-reasons-to-care-about-education-for-refugees/. Accessed March 15, 2021.

108. UNHCR, www.unhcr.org/en-us/teaching-about-refugees.html. Accessed March 15, 2021.

109. UNHCR, Teaching About Refugees, www.unhcr.org/en-us/teaching-about-refugees.html. Accessed March 15, 2021.

110. San Diego County has the largest concentration of refugees in California. Since 2000, the county has consistently received more refugee arrivals than any other region in the state. The trend dates to the late 1970s, when some 50,000 Southeast Asian refugees passed through Camp Pendleton in the months following the fall of Saigon. Many of these refugees settled in San Diego, helping make the area, especially the City Heights neighborhood, an important hub for the resettlement of refugees and paving the path for Burmese, East African, Iraqi, Syrian, and other refugees arriving in San Diego today. Since 1975, more than 85,000 refugees have made San Diego County their first home. See McLaren and Wood 2017. During federal fiscal year 2016, the year immediately preceding our symposium, more than 3,000 refugees resettled in San Diego County, compelling area schools, many already operating with limited

resources, to scramble to deliver quality education for newcomer students and their families.

111. Planning the two-day conference took months, as our team conferred with a long list of stakeholders. Teachers' buy-in was key. We met with a number of teachers in the San Diego Unified School District, partnered with the San Diego Education Association, and worked with the University of California, San Diego, Extension to provide professional development credit (1.5 quarter units) for teachers who attended the symposium. We ensured participation by local refugees by consulting with community leaders, personally inviting community members, offering childcare for attendees, and providing translation services, as needed. We paid all our speakers and performers and offered transportation and translation services to all refugee student and parent speakers.

112. Building on the momentum of the Refugee Teaching Symposium, the CRSC applied and received the 2020–21 Whiting Public Engagement Fellowship to launch the Refugee Teaching Institute (RTI), a series of public workshops that bring high school teachers together with refugee students and parents, and a broader public, to collaborate on lesson plans that center refugees' histories and worldviews. Led by CRSC Founding Member, Ma Vang, the RTI is a public-facing four-workshop series designed to craft long-term initiatives on refugee teaching in Merced in California's Central Valley.

113. Nguyen 2013.

114. Hatton 2016, 126.

115. Abumaye 2017.

116. Hatton 2017.

117. Adichi 2013.

118. Vuong 2019, 231.

4   A Refugee Critique of Representations: On Criticality and Creativity

1. Soguk 2007, 294.

2. Naimou 2016, 227.

3. Herman and Chomsky 2006, 1.

4. McChesney 2008, 435.

5. Wasko 2014, 261.

6. Adichie 2009.

7. Hatton 2018, 127.

8. Hong 2020b, 91.

9. Quoted in Sharif 2019b, 9.

10. Um 2015, 213.

11. Um 2017.

12. Nguyen 2019, 111.

13. Vang 2016, 30.

14. Nguyen 2018, 20.

15. Nguyen 2018, 20.

16. Quoted in Teicher 2016.

17. See Richey 2015; Chouliaraki 2012.

18. Du Bois 1968, 2–3.

19. Snow 2020, 168.

20. Quoted in Laurent 2015.

21. Willis 2019, 104.

22. Manchanda 2004, 4179.

23. Willis 2019, 103.

24. Bouckaert, in Laurent 2015.

25. Wright 2002, 54.

26. Rangan 2017, 3.

27. Agamben 1998.

28. Rajaram 2002, 247.

29. Rajaram 2002, 251.

30. Malkki 1996, 379.

31. Snow 2020, 167.

32. Yue 2008, 240-4`1.

33. Koçak 2020, 30.

34. Jung 2015, 312.

35. Puar 2006, 85.

36. Luibhéid 2008, 180.

37. Stonebridge 2018, 23.

38. Blazan 2018, 181.

39. Kaplan 2006, 708.

40. Chow 2006.

41. Fernandes 2013, 193

42. Hyndman 2010, 90; Lubkemann 2008, 36.

43. Espiritu and Duong 2018, 590.

44. Tuck 2009, 416.

45. Quoted in Thor 2015.

46. Quoted in Thor 2015.

47. Ku, Manalansan, and Mannur 2013, 5.

48. Sharif 2019a, 2-3.

49. Sharif 2019a, 17.

50. Duong 2020, 56.

51. Nguyen 2020, 229.

52. Bui 2016, 110.

53. Gordon 1997, 4-5.

54. Foundland Collective 2015.

55. Moraga and Anzaldúa 1981.

56. Derrida 1995, 33-4.

57. Trouillot 1995, 48.

58. Qasmiyeh 2020, 55.

59. Vang 2021, 10.

Conclusion: In/Verse

1. Sharpe 2019.

2. Layoun 1995.

3. Gumbs 2012.

4. We borrow this phrase from Claudine Rankine's book, *Just Us: An American Conversation* (2020).

5. Imarisha et al. 2017.

References

Abulhawa, Susan. 2006. *Mornings in Jenin.* New York: Bloomsbury USA.

Abumaye, Mohamed. 2017. "Askar: Militarism, Policing, and Somali Refugees." PhD dissertation, University of California, San Diego.

Adichie, Chimamanda Ngozi. 2009. "The Danger of a Single Story." TED: Ideas Worth Spreading. www.ted.com/talks/chimamanda_adichie_the_danger_of_a_single_story.html.

Aguilar, Felix. 2017. "The People vs. Us." In *The Wandering Song: Central American Writing in the United States,* edited by Leticia Hernandez Linares, 78–79. Sylmar, CA: Tia Chucha Press.

Akee, Randall. 2020. "COVID-19 Impact on Indigenous Peoples in the U.S." EconoFact, May 12. Accessed July 20, 2020. https://econofact.org/covid-19-impact-on-indigenous-peoples-in-the-u.-s.

Akram, Susan. 2014. "UNRWA and Palestinian Refugees." In *The Oxford Handbook of Refugee and Forced Migration Studies,* 244–55. Oxford: Oxford University Press.

Arar, Rawan. 2018. "Leveraging Sovereignty: Jordan and the Syrian Refugee Crisis." PhD dissertation, University of California, San Diego.

Astles, Jacinta. 2020. "Migrant Caravans: Explained." *On the Move,* January 31. https://rosanjose.iom.int/SITE/en/blog/migrant-caravans-explained.

Atanasoski, Neda. 2013. *Humanitarian Violence: The U.S. Deployment of Diversity.* Minneapolis: University of Minnesota Press.

Bacon, Katie. 2000. "An African Voice." *The Atlantic,* August 8. www.theatlantic.com/magazine/archive/2000/08/an-african-voice/306020.

Baldwin, James. 1992. *The Fire Next Time.* New York: Vintage.

Barboza, Tony, and Ben Poston. 2020. "'I Was Naive to Think This Couldn't Touch My Family': Pacific Islanders Hit Hard by the Coronavirus." *Los Angeles Times*, July 19. Accessed July 28, 2020. www.latimes.com /california/story/2020-07-19/california-pacific-islander-native-hawaiian-communities-hit-hard-by-coronavirus.

Barnett, Laura. 2002. "Global Governance and the Evolution of the International Refugee Regime." *International Journal of Refugee Law* 14 (2–3): 238–62.

Barnett, Michael. 1995. "The New U.N. Politics of Peace: From Juridical Sovereignty to Empirical Sovereignty." *Global Governance* 1 (1): 79–97.

Beech, Hannah, and Ben Hubbard. 2020. "Unprepared for the Worst: World's Most Vulnerable Brace for Virus." *New York Times*, March 26. Accessed July 28, 2020. www.nytimes.com/2020/03/26/world/asia/coronavirus-refugees-camps-bangladesh.html.

Beltrán, Cristina. 2021. "To Understand Trump's Support, We Must Think in Terms of Multiracial Whiteness." *Washington Post*, January 15. Accessed January 15, 2021. https://www.washingtonpost.com/opinions/2021/01/15 /understand-trumps-support-we-must-think-terms-multiracial-whiteness/.

Benjamin, Walter. 1973. "Theses on the Philosophy of History." In *Illuminations,* edited by Hannah Arendt, 245–55. London: Collins/Fontana.

Blazan, Sladja. 2018. "Literature and the Agency of the Refugee: An Analysis of Narrative Structures Employed in Elfriede Jelinek's *Die Schutzbefohlenen* and Viet Thanh Nguyen's *The Refugees.*" In *Refugees and/in Literature,* edited by Sladja Blazan and Nigel Hatton, 171–92. Würzburg, Germany: Königshausen & Neumann.

Blazan, Sladja, and Nigel Hatton. 2016. "Introduction: Refugees and/in Literature." In *Refugees and/in Literature,* edited by Sladja Blazan and Nigel Hatton, 97–118. Würzburg: Königshausen & Neumann.

Buchanan, Larry, Quoctrung Bui, and Jugal K. Patel. 2020. "Black Lives Matter May Be the Largest Movement in U.S. History." *New York Times*, July 3. Accessed July 20, 2020. www.nytimes.com/interactive /2020/07/03/us/george-floyd-protests-crowd-size.html.

Bui, Long. 2016. "The Refugee Repertoire: Performing and Staging the Postmemories of Violence." *MELUS* 41 (3): 112–32.

———. 2018. *Returns of War: South Vietnam and the Price of Refugee Memory.* New York: New York University Press.

Bulawayo, NoViolet. 2013. *We Need New Names.* New York: Reagan Arthur Books.

Butler, Judith. 2006. *Precarious Life: The Powers of Mourning and Violence.* London: Verso Books.

Cafferty, Helen, and Jeanette Clausen. 1998. "What's Feminist about It? Reflections on Collaboration in Editing and Writing." In *Common Ground: Feminist Collaboration in the Academy,* edited by Elizabeth Peck and JoAnna Stephens Mink, 81–98. New York: State University of New York Press.

Carruthers, Susan L. 2005. "Between Camps: Eastern Bloc 'Escapees' and Cold War Borderlands." *American Quarterly* 57: 911–42.

Casavantes Bradford, Anita. 2018. "Immigrants, Refugees, and American Family Values: A Historical Reckoning." Critical Refugee Studies, July 16. https://criticalrefugeestudies.com/blog/immigrants-refugees-and-american-family-values-a-historical-reckoning.

———. 2019a. "'Another Foothold in Our Fight against Communism': Race, Religion, and Public Relations in the Hungarian and Cuban Refugee Programs, 1956–1961." *U.S. Catholic Historian* 37 (3): 43–76.

———. 2019b. "Suffer the Little Children: Unaccompanied Child Migrants and the Geopolitics of Compassion in 20th Century America: Insights from a Work in Progress." Paper presented at the Center for Comparative Immigration Studies, University of California, San Diego, December 2.

Cheatham, Amelia. 2019. "Central America's Turbulent Northern Triangle." Council on Foreign Relations, October 1. www.cfr.org/backgrounder /central-americas-turbulent-northern-triangle.

Chouliaraki, Lilie. 2012. "The Theatricality of Humanitarianism: A Critique of Celebrity Advocacy." *Communication and Critical/Cultural Studies* 9 (1): 1–21.

Chow, Rey. 2006. *The Age of the World Target: Self-Referentiality in War, Theory, and Comparative Work.* Durham, NC: Duke University Press.

Cohn, D'vera, Jeffrey S. Passel, and Ana Gonzalez-Barrera. 2017. "Rise in U.S. Immigrants from El Salvador, Guatemala and Honduras Outpaces

Growth from Elsewhere." Pew Research, December 7. www.pewresearch
.org/hispanic/2017/12/07/rise-in-u-s-immigrants-from-el-salvador-
guatemala-and-honduras-outpaces-growth-from-elsewhere/.

Congressional Research Service. 2019. "Unaccompanied Alien Children: An
Overview." October 9. https://fas.org/sgp/crs/homesec/R43599.pdf.

Covid Data Tracker. 2021. Centers for Disease Control, January 18. Accessed
January 19, 2021. https://covid.cdc.gov/covid-data-tracker/#cases_
totalcases.

Critical Refugee Studies. 2020. "Critical Vocabularies." https://criticalrefu-
geestudies.com/resources/critical-vocabularies.

Critical Refugee Studies Collective. n.d. "Refuge." criticalrefugeestudies.
com/resources/critical-vocabularies.

Das, Venna. 2006. *Life and Words: Violence and the Descent into the Ordinary*.
Berkeley: University of California Press.

Day, Iyko. 2020. "The Yellow Plague and Romantic Anticapitalism." *Monthly
Review* 72 (3): 64–73.

De Genova, Nicholas. 2010a. "The Deportation Regime: Sovereignty, Space,
and the Freedom of Movement." In *The Deportation Regime: Sovereignty,
Space and the Freedom of Movement*, edited by Nicholas de Genova and
Nathalie Peutz, 33–65. Durham, NC: Duke University Press.

———. 2010b. "The Queer Politics of Migration: Reflections on 'Illegality'
and Incorrigibility." *Studies in Social Justice* 4 (2): 101–26.

Dempster, Helen, Thomas Ginn, Jimmy Graham, Martha Guerrero Ble, Daphne
Jayasinghe, and Barri Shorey. 2020. "Locked Down and Left Behind: The
Impact of COVID-19 on Refugees' Economic Inclusion." Center for Global
Development, Refugees International, International Rescue Committee,
July 8. Accessed July 28, 2020. www.refugeesinternational.org/reports
/2020/7/6/locked-down-and-left-behind-the-impact-of-covid-19-on-
refugees-economic-inclusion.

Derrida, Jacques. 1995. *Archive Fever: A Freudian Impression*. Chicago:
University of Chicago Press.

Dessalegne, Damtew, and Eliza Savvidou. 2015. "Do Not Conflate Refugees
with Terrorists." United Nations High Commissioner for Refugees. www
.unhcr.org/cy/wp-content/uploads/sites/41/2015/12/JointStatementUN-
HCR-Ombudswoman_Dec2015.pdf.

Dickerson, Caitlin. 2020. "Inside the Refugee Camp on America's Doorstep." *New York Times,* October 23. www.nytimes.com/2020/10/23/us/mexico-migrant-camp-asylum.html.

Du Bois, W. E. B. 1968. *The Souls of Black Folk: Essays and Sketches.* New York: Johnson Reprint Corp.

Duong, Lan. 2020. "Archives of Memory: Vietnamese American Films, Past and Present." *Film Quarterly* 73 (3): 54–58.

Erakat, Noura. 2019. *Justice for Some: Law and the Question of Palestine.* Stanford, CA: Stanford University Press.

Espiritu, Yến Lê. 2014. *Body Counts: The Vietnam War and Militarized Refugees.* Berkeley: University of California Press.

Espiritu, Yến Lê, and Lan Duong. 2018. "Feminist Refugee Epistemology: Reading Displacement in Vietnamese and Syrian Art." *Signs* 43 (3): 587–615.

Espiritu, Yến Lê, and J. A. Ruanto-Ramirez. 2020. "The Philippine Refugee Processing Center: The Relational Displacements of Vietnamese Refugees and the Indigenous Aetas." *Verge: Studies in Global Asias* 6 (1): 118–41.

Euro-Mediterranean Human Rights Monitor. 2021. "Inescapable Hell: The Israeli military attack on the Gaza Strip (May 10–21, 2021)." https://euromedmonitor.org/uploads/reports/gazareporteng.pdf.

European Civil Protection and Humanitarian Aid Operations. 2020. "EU's Humanitarian Aid for 2020." November 26. https://ec.europa.eu/echo/funding-evaluations/funding-humanitarian-aid_en.

"Family Separation under the Trump Administration—a Timeline." 2020. *Features and Stories,* June 17. Accessed February 27, 2020. https://www.splcenter.org/news/2020/06/17/family-separation-under-trump-administration-timeline#2020.

Fassin, Didier. 2012. *Humanitarian Reason: A Moral History of the Present.* Berkeley: University of California Press.

Fee, Molly, and Rawan Arar. 2019. "What Happens When the United States Stops Taking in Refugees?" *Contexts* 18 (2): 18–23.

Feldman, Ilana. 2018. *Life Lived in Relief: Humanitarian Predicaments and Palestinian Refugee Politics.* Oakland: University of California Press.

Fernandes, Leela. 2013. *Transnational Feminism in the United States: Knowledge, Ethics, and Power.* New York: New York University Press.

Flagg, Anna, and Andrew R. Calderon. 2020. "500,000 Kids, 30 Million Hours: Trump's Vast Expansion of Child Detention." The Marshall Project, October 30. www.themarshallproject.org/2020/10/30/500-000-kids-30-million-hours-trump-s-vast-expansion-of-child-detention.

Foundland Collective. 2015. "Artist Statement." Accessed September 31, 2016. http://foundland.info/ABOUT.

Global Internal Displacement Database. www.internaldisplacement.org /database/displacement-data.

Gordon, Avery F. 1997. *Ghostly Matters: Haunting and the Sociological Imagination*. Minneapolis: University of Minnesota Press.

Grandi, Filippo. 2020. "Statement to the Third Committee of the United Nations General Assembly." November 3. www.unhcr.org/admin /hcspeeches/5fa19c0f4/statement-third-committee-united-nations-general-assembly.html.

Gregory, Derek. 2004. "Part 5: Barbed Boundaries." In *The Colonial Present: Afghanistan, Palestine, Iraq*, 76–106. New York: Blackwell.

Gumbs, Alexis Pauline. 2012. "The Shape of My Impact." The Feminist Wire, October 29 Accessed December 1, 2020. https://thefeministwire.com /2012/10/the-shape-of-my-impact/.

Güner, Ezgi. 2019. "What Is the Racial in Racial Capitalism? Magic, Partition, Politics: A Lecture by Ruth Wilson Gilmore (Gradual Center CUNY)—Response by Ezni Guner." April 3. Accessed July 28, 2020. https:// unitforcriticism.wordpress.com/2019/04/03/what-is-the-racial-in-racial-capitalism-magic-partition-politics-a-lecture-by-ruth-wilson-gilmore-grad-center-cuny-response-by-ezgi-guner-anthropology/.

Haidari, Karim. 2002. "08:59." *New Internationalist*, no. 350 (October). https://newint.org/features/2002/10/05/journey.

Hamdi, Tahrir. 2011. "Bearing Witness in Palestinian Resistance Literature." *Race & Class* 52 (3): 21–42.

Hassouri, Parastou. 2003. "War on Terrorism Is Like a War on Immigrants." ACLU-NJ. www.aclu-nj.org/theissues/immigrantrights /waronterrorismislikewaroni.

Hatton, Nigel. 2016. "Post-Homeric Odyssey: Reimagining the Fictional Space between Human Rights Advocates and the Poor, Dehumanized and

Uprooted." In *Refugees and/in Literature,* edited by Sladja Blazan and Nigel Hatton, 121–34. Würzburg: Königshausen & Neumann.

———. 2017. "Refugee Lifeworlds: Classroom Exercises on Dignity, Solidarity and Possibility." Keynote speech, Refugee Teaching Symposium, San Diego, CA, November 4.

———. 2018. "Post-Homeric Odyssey: Reimagining the Fictional Space Between Human Rights Advocates and the Poor, Dehumanized and Uprooted." In *Refugees and/in Literature,* edited by Sladja Blazan and Nigel Hatton, 121–134. Würzburg: Königshausen & Neumann.

Herman, Edward, and Noam Chomsky. 2006. "A Propaganda Model." In *Media and Cultural Studies: Keyworks,* edited by Meenakshi Gigi Durham and Douglas M. Kellner, 257–94. Malden, MA: Blackwell.

Hong, Mai-Linh. 2017. "Narrative in the Shadow of the Refugee Regime." *The Account: A Journal of Poetry, Prose, and Thought* 9. www.theaccountmagazine.com.

———. 2020a. "Navigating the Global Refugee Regime: Law, Myth, Story." *Amerasia Journal* 46 (1): 34–48.

———. 2020b. "The Refugee's Now: The Art and Advocacy of Matt Huynh." *Verge: Studies in Global Asias* 6 (1):86–103.

Hope, Jeanelle K. 2019. "'This Tree Needs Water!': A Case Study on the Radical Potential of Afro-Asian Solidarity in the Era of Black Lives Matter." *Amerasia Journal* 45 (2): 1–16. DOI:10.1080/00447471.2019.1684807.

Hyndman, Jennifer. 2000. *Managing Displacement: Refugees and the Politics of Humanitarianism.* Minneapolis: University of Minnesota Press.

———. 2010. "Introduction: The Feminist Politics of Refugee Migration." *Gender, Place, and Culture* 17 (4): 453–59.

Imarisha, Walidah, Alexis Gumbs, Leah Lakshmi Piepzna-Samarsinha, Adrienne Maree Brown, and Mia Mingus. 2017. "The Fictions and Futures of Transformative Justice." The New Inquiry, April 20. Accessed December 1, 2020. https://thenewinquiry.com/the-fictions-and-futures-of-transformative-justice/.

Jasser, M. Zuhdi. 2014. "Sectarian Conflict in Syria." PRISM 4: 56–87. Syria Supplement.

Jayawardhan, Shweta. 2017. "Vulnerability and Climate Change Induced Human Displacement." *Consilience* 17: 105, 115.

Jones, Angela. 2013. "Introduction: Queer Utopias, Queer Futurity, and Potentiality in Quotidian Practice." In *A Critical Inquiry into Queer Utopias,* edited by Angela Jones, 1–20. New York: Palgrave Macmillan.

Jung, Mariska. 2015. "Logics of Citizenship and Violence of Rights: The Queer Migrant Body and the Asylum System." *Birkbeck Law Review* 3 (2): 305–35.

Kaplan, Caren. 2006. "Precision Targets: GPS and the Militarization of U.S. Consumer Identity." *American Quarterly* 58 (3): 693–713.

Karell, Linda. 2002. *Writing Together, Writing Apart.* Lincoln: University of Nebraska Press.

Kestler-D'Amours, Jillian. 2021. "The Trump-Era Order Biden Is Using to Turn Away Most Migrants." *Aljazeera*, April 7. www.aljazeera.com/news/2021/4/7/the-trump-era-rule-biden-is-using-to-turn-asylum-seekers-away.

Klaas, Sunčica. 2016. "'We Will Give Him a Family': Economies of Race and Rescue in the Autobiographies of Young African Refugees." In *Refugees and/in Literature,* edited by Sladja Blazan and Nigel Hatton, 193–206. Würzburg: Königshausen & Neumann.

Koçak, Mert. 2020. "Who Is 'Queerer' and Deserves Resettlement? Queer Asylum Seekers and Their Deservingness of Refugee Status in Turkey." *Middle East Critique* 29 (1): 31.

Kondo, Dorinne. 2018. *Worldmaking: Race, Performance, and the Work of Creativity.* Durham, NC: Duke University Press.

Kopan, Tal. 2018. "DHS: 2,000 Children Separated from Parents at Border." CNN, June 16. www.cnn.com/2018/06/15/politics/dhs-family-separation-numbers/index.html.

Krug, Nora. 2018. "A Moment on 'Oprah' Made Her a Human Rights Symbol. She Wants to Be More than That." *Washington Post,* April 19.

Ku, Robert, Martin Manalansan IV, and Anita Mannur. 2013. "An Alimentary Introduction." In *Eating Asian America: A Food Studies Reader,* edited by Robert Ku, Martin Manalansan IV, and Anita Mannur, 1–12. New York: New York University Press.

Laurent, Olivier. 2015. "What the Image of Aylan Kurdi Says about the Power of Photography." *Time*, September 4. Accessed November 13, 2016. https://time.com/4022765/aylan-kurdi-photo/.

Layoun, Mary. 1995. "(Mis)trusting Narratives: Refugee Stories of Post-1922 Greece and Post-1974 Cyprus." In *Mistrusting Refugees,* edited by E. Valentine Daniel and John Chr. Knudsen, 73–86. Berkeley: University of California Press.

Leenders, Reinoud. 2010. "Getting the 'Ladder of Options' Right—the Illusive and Real Security Fallout of the Iraqi Refugee Crisis." *Middle East Institute—Fondation pour la Recherche Stratégique,* September 15.

lê thi diem thúy. 2003. *The Gangster We Are All Looking For.* New York: Knopf.

Lipman, Jana K. 2012. "'Give Us a Ship': The Vietnamese Repatriate Movement on Guam, 1975." *American Quarterly* 64: 1–31.

———. 2020. *In Camps: Vietnamese Refugees, Asylum Seekers, and Repatriates.* Oakland: University of California Press.

Lippert, Randy. 1999. "Governing Refugees: The Relevance of Governmentality to Understanding the International Refugee Regime." *Alternatives: Global, Local, Political* 24: 295–328.

Liu, Robyn. 2002. "Governing Refugees 1919-1945. " *Borderlands e-journal* 1 (1). www.borderlands.net.au.

Lorde, Audre. 1980. *The Cancer Journals.* San Francisco: Aunt Lute.

———. 1984. "The Master's Tools Will Never Dismantle the Master's House." In *Sister Outsider: Essays and Speeches,* 110–14. Trumansburg, NY: Crossing Press, 1984.

Lubkemann, Stephen C. 2008. *Culture in Chaos: An Anthropology of the Social Condition of War.* Chicago: University of Chicago Press.

Luibhéid, Eithne. 2008. "Queer/Migration: An Unruly Body of Scholarship." *GLQ: A Journal of Lesbian & Gay Studies* 14 (2-3): 169–90.

Malkki, Lisa. 1996. "Speechless Emissaries: Refugees, Humanitarianism, and Dehistoricization." *Cultural Anthropology* 11 (3): 377–404.

Manchanda, Rita. 2004. "Gender, Conflict, and Displacement: Contesting 'Infantilisation' of Forced Migrant Women." *Economic and Political Weekly* 39 (37): 4179–86.

Marshall, Serena. 2016. "Obama Has Deported More People than Any Other President." *ABC News*, August 29. Accessed December 20, 2020. https://abcnews.go.com/Politics/obamas-deportation-policy-numbers/story?id=41715661.

McChesney, Robert W. 2008. *The Political Economy of Media: Enduring Issues, Emerging Dilemmas.* New York: Monthly Review Press.

McFarling, Usha Lee. 2020. "Nursing Ranks Are Filled with Filipino Americans: The Pandemic Is Taking an Outsized Toll on Them." STAT, April 28. Accessed July 20, 2020. www.statnews.com/2020/04/28 /coronavirus-taking-outsized-toll-on-filipino-american-nurses/.

McGranahan, Carole. 2016. "Theorizing Refusal: An Introduction." *Cultural Anthropology* 31 (3): 319–25.

McLaren, Mandy, and Megan Wood. 2017. "Trauma and Transitions: How San Diego Grapples with Educating Refugees." Inewsource, August 28. https://inewsource.org/2017/08/28/educating-Refugees/.

McNevin, Anne. 2013. "Ambivalence and Citizenship: Theorizing the Political Claims of Irregular Migrants." *Millennium: Journal of International Studies* 41 (2): 182–200.

Mertus, J. 1998. "The State and the Post–Cold War Refugee Regime: New Models, New Questions." *International Journal of Refugee Law* 10 (3): 320–47.

Mignolo, Walter D. 2009. "Epistemic Disobedience, Independent Thought and Decolonial Freedom." *Theory, Culture and Society* 26 (708): 159–81.

Miroff, Nick. 2020. "As U.S. Expels Migrants, They Return, Again and Again, across Mexico Border. *Washington Post*, August 9.

Moraga, Cherríe, and Gloria Anzaldúa. 1981. *This Bridge Called My Back: Writings by Radical Women of Color.* New York: Kitchen Table/Women of Color Press.

Muller, Tanja R. 2013. "The Long Shadow of Band Aid Humanitarianism: Revisiting the Dynamics between Famine and Celebrity." *Third World Quarterly* 33 (4): 470–84.

Muñoz, José Esteban. 2009. *Cruising Utopia: The Then and There of Queer Futurity.* New York: New York University Press.

Musarat-Akram, Susan. 1999. "The World Refugee Regime in Crisis: A Failure to Fulfill the Burden-Sharing and Humanitarian Requirements of the 1951 Refugee Convention." *Proceedings of the Annual Meeting (American Society of International Law)* 93: 213–16.

Naimou, Angela. 2016. "Double Vision: Refugee Crises and the Afterimages of Endless War." *College Literature: A Journal of Critical Literary Studies* 43 (1): 226–33.

Nayeri, Dina. 2017. "The Ungrateful Refugee: 'We Have No Debt to Repay.'" *The Guardian*, April 4. www.theguardian.com/world/2017/apr/04 /dina-nayeri-ungrateful-Refugee.

———. 2019. *The Ungrateful Refugee: What Immigrants Never Tell You.* New York: Catapult.

Neal, Joan. 2020. "Being Black and Immigrant in America." August 3. Accessed August 20, 2021. https://cmsny.org/being-black-and-immigrant-in-america/.

Nebehay, Stephanie. 2014. "Syrian Refugees, Sectarian Tensions Endanger Lebanon: U.N." Reuters, July 14. www.reuters.com/article/us-syria-crisis-lebanon-un/syrian-refugees-sectarian-tensions-endanger-lebanon-u-n-idUSKBN0FJ1RJ20140714.

Nguyen, Ly Thuy. 2020. "Queer Dis/Inheritance and Refugee Futures." *WSQ: Women's Studies Quarterly* 48 (1–2): 218–35.

Nguyen, Mimi Thi. 2012. *The Gift of Freedom: War, Debt, and Other Refugee Passages.* Durham, NC: Duke University Press.

Nguyen, Viet Thanh. 2016. "The Hidden Scars We All Carry." *New York Times*, September 2. Accessed September 15, 2020. www.nytimes. com/2016/09/03/opinion/the-hidden-scars-all-refugees-carry.html.

———. 2018. "Introduction: The Displaced." In *The Displaced,* edited by Viet Thanh Nguyen, 11–22. New York: Abrams Press.

Nguyen, Vinh. 2013. "Refugee Gratitude: Narrating Success and Intersubjectivity in Kim Thuy's *Ru*." *Contested Migrations: Special Issue of Canadian Literature* 219 (Winter): 17–36.

———. 2019. "Refugeetude: When Does a Refugee Stop Being a Refugee?" *Social Text* 37 (2): 109–31.

"9 Quotes by Refugees." 2017. June 23. https://peacebuildingsolutions.org /refugee-quotes/.

Nowrasteh, Alex. 2020. "21 People Died in Immigration Detention in 2020." *CATO Institute Blog,* October 22. www.cato.org/blog/21-people-died-immigration-detention-2020.

"Ocean Vuong on Race, Sexuality, and His New Novel." 2019. Interview by Christiane Amanpour. *Amanpour & Co.,* PBS, October 31.

Ogata, Sadako. 1951. Foreword to "The Refugee Convention, 1951." United Nations High Commissioner for Refugees. Accessed February 1, 2021. www.unhcr.org/4ca34be29.pdf.

Oh, Arissa H. 2012. "From War Waif to Ideal Immigrant: The Cold War Transformation of The Korean Orphan." *Journal of American Ethnic History* 31 (4): 34–55.

Ong, Aihwa. 2003. *Buddha Is Hiding: Refugees, Citizenship, the New America.* Berkeley: University of California Press.

Oppel, Richard, Robert Gebeloff, Rebecca Lai, Will Wright, and Mitch Smith. 2020. "The Fullest Look Yet at the Racial Inequality of Coronavirus." *New York Times*, July 5. Accessed July 20, 2020. www.nytimes.com /interactive/2020/07/05/us/coronavirus-latinos-african-americans-cdc-data.html.

Paik, Naomi A. 2020. *Bans, Walls, Raids, Sanctuary: Understanding U.S. Immigration for the Twenty-First Century.* Oakland: University of California Press.

Peteet, Julie. 2010. "Cartographic Violence, Displacement and Refugee Camps: Palestine and Iraq." In *Palestinian Refugees,* edited by Are Knudsen and Sari Anafi, 13–28. New York: Routledge.

Pew Research Center. 2021. "Key Facts about U.S. Immigration Policies and Biden's Proposed Changes." March 22. www.pewresearch.org/fact-tank/2022/01/11/key-facts-about-u-s-immigration-policies-and-bidens-proposed-changes/.

Pirtle, Whitney N. Laster. 2020. "Racial Capitalism: A Fundamental Cause of Novel Coronavirus (COVID-19) Pandemic Inequities in the United States." *Health Education & Behavior* 47 (4): 504–8.

Pooja, Rangan. 2017. *Immediations: The Humanitarian Impulse in Documentary.* Durham, NC: Duke University Press.

Poujoulat, Anne-Christine. 2020. "Protests across the Globe after George Floyd's Death." CNN, June 13. Accessed June 20, 2020. www.cnn .com/2020/06/06/world/gallery/intl-george-floyd-protests/index.html.

"Poul Hartling Quotes." *AZ Quotes.* www.azquotes.com/author/20463-Poul_ Hartling.

Puar, Jasbir. 2007. *Terrorist Assemblages: Homonationalism in Queer Times.* Durham, NC: Duke University Press.

———. 2008. "Mapping U.S. Homonormativities." *Gender, Place, and Culture: A Journal of Feminist Geography* 13 (1): 67–88.

Qasmiyeh, Yousif M. 2020. "Writing the Camp, Writing the Camp Archive: The Case of Baddawi Refugee Camp in Lebanon." In *Refuge in a Moving World,* edited by Elena Fiddian-Qasmiyeh, 52–73. London: UCL Press.

Quintanilla, Olivia Arlene. 2020. "Inafa' Maolek Restoring Balance through Resilience, Resistance, and Coral Reefs: A Study of Pacific Island Climate Justice and the Right to Nature." PhD dissertation, University of California, San Diego.

Qutami, Loubna, and Omar Zahzah. 2020. "The War of Words: Language as an Instrument of Palestinian National Liberation." *Arab Studies Quarterly* 42 (1–2): 66–90.

Rajaram, Prem Kumar. 2002. "Humanitarianism and Representations of the Refugee." *Journal of Refugee Studies* 15 (3): 247–64.

Rangan, Pooja. 2017. *Immediations: The Humanitarian Impulse in Documentary.* Durham, NC: Duke University Press.

Rankine, Claudia. 2020. *Just Us: An American Conversation.* New York: Graywolf Press.

Rempel, Terry M. 2000. *The United Nations Conciliation Commission for Palestine, Protection, and a Durable Solution for Palestinian Refugees.* Information & Discussion Brief, Issue No. 5, BADIL, June.

Reucher, Gaby. 2019. "The Dignity of Refugees: Homi K. Bhabha Speaks at the Ruhrtriennale." *DW*, September 16. www.dw.com/en/the-dignity-of-refugees-homi-k-bhabha-speaks-at-the-ruhrtriennale/a-50447227.

Richey, Lisa. 2015. *Celebrity Humanitarianism and North-South Relations: Politics, Place, and Power.* New York: Routledge.

Roy, Arundhati. 2020. "The Pandemic Is a Portal." *Financial Times*, April 3. Accessed April 3, 2020. www.ft.com/content/10d8f5e8-74eb-11ea-95fe-fcd274e920ca.

Said, Edward. 1990. "Reflections on Exile." *Out There: Marginalization and Contemporary Cultures,* edited by Russell Ferguson, Martha Gever, Trinh T. Minh-ha, and Cornel West, 357–66. Cambridge, MA: MIT Press.

Sharif, Lila. 2014. "Savory Politics: Land, Memory, and the Ecological Occupation of Palestine." PhD dissertation, University of California, San Diego.

———. 2019a. "'Because Food Is the Essence of the Everyday'; Or, the Palestinian Hearth and Everyday Survival." Unpublished manuscript, November 21.

———. 2019b. "'The Permanent Sense of the Diaspora in My Body': Narrating Resistance and Displacement in Mary Hazboun's 'Art of Weeping' through a Feminist Refugee Epistemology." Unpublished manuscript, November 21.

Sharpe, Christina. 2019. "Beauty Is a Method." *e-flux* 105 (December). Accessed December 1, 2020. www.e-flux.com/journal/105/303916/beauty-is-a-method/.

Simpson, Audra. 2007. "On Ethnographic Refusal: Indigeneity, 'Voice' and Colonial Citizenship." *Junctures* 9: 67–80.

———. 2014. *Mohawk Interruptus: Political Life across the Border of Settler States*. Durham, NC: Duke University Press.

———. 2017. "The Use of Consent and the Anatomy of 'Refusal': Cases from Indigenous North America and Australia." *Postcolonial Studies* 20 (1): 18–33. DOI:10.1080/13688790.2017.1334283.

Smith, Tracy K. "The United States Welcomes You." In *Wade in the Water*. New York: Graywolf Press, 2018. Reprinted at www.poetryfoundation.org/poems/147469/the-united-states-welcomes-you.

Snow, Tom. 2020. "Visual Politics and the 'Refugee' Crisis: The Images of Alan Kurdi." In *Refuge in a Moving World*, edited by Elena Fiddian-Qasmiyeh, 166–76. London: UCL Press.

Soguk, Nevzat. 1999. *States and Strangers: Refugees and Displacements of Statecraft*. Minneapolis: University of Minnesota Press.

———. 2007. "Border's Capture: Insurrectional Politics, Border-Crossing Humans, and the New Political." In *Borderscapes: Hidden Geographies and Politics at Territory's Edge*, edited by Prem Kumar Rajaram and Carl Grundy-Warr, 283–308. Minneapolis: University of Minnesota Press.

Stack, Megan K. 2000. "Behrouz Boochani Just Wants to Be Free." *New York Times Magazine*, August 4. www.nytimes.com/2020/08/04/magazine/behrouz-boochani-australia.html.

Stevenson, Lisa. 2014. *Life Beside Itself: Imagining Care in the Canadian Arctic*. Berkeley: University of California Press.

Stonebridge, Lindsay. 2018. *Placeless People: Writings, Rights, and Refugees*. Oxford: Oxford University Press.

Sturken, Marita. 1997. *Tangled Memories: The Vietnam War, the AIDS Epidemic, and the Politics of Remembering.* Berkeley: University of California Press.

Swain, Jon. 1995. *River of Time: A Memoir of Vietnam and Cambodia.* New York: St. Martin's Press.

Tang, Eric. 2015. *Unsettled: Cambodian Refugees in the New York City Hyperghetto.* Philadelphia: Temple University Press.

Tang, Terry. 2021. "Victims of Anti-Asian Attacks Reflect a Year into the Pandemic." *PBS News Hour*, March 2. Accessed March 4, 2021. www.pbs.org/newshour/nation/victims-of-anti-asian-attacks-reflect-a-year-into-pandemic.

Teicher, Jordan. 2016. "Here's What the Everyday Lives of Refugees Look Like." *Slate*, May 4. Accessed June 30, 2016. https://slate.com/culture/2016/05/Refugee-from-the-annenberg-space-for-photographys-exhibit-shows-the-global-migration-crisis.html.

Temp, Carl J. Bon. 2008. *Americans at the Gate: The United States and Refugees during the Cold War.* Princeton, NJ: Princeton University Press.

Thor, Rebecka. 2015. "Ten Questions: Nisrine Boukhari." *Kunstrkritikk*, November 29. Accessed September 31, 2016. www.kunstkritikk.com/artikler/10-questions-nisrine-boukhari/.

Trouillot, Michel-Rolph. 1995. *Silencing the Past: Power and the Production of History.* Boston: Beacon Press.

Trump, Donald J. 2017. "Inaugural Address." Washington, DC, January 20. Accessed July 28, 2020. www.whitehouse.gov/briefings-statements/the-inaugural-address/.

Tuck, Eve. 2009. "Suspending Damage: A Letter to Communities." *Harvard Educational Review* 79 (3): 409–28.

Um, Khatharya. 2015. *From the Land of Shadows: War, Revolution, and the Making of the Cambodian Diaspora.* New York: New York University Press.

———. 2017. "Critical Vocabularies: Refugitude." Accessed July 29, 2020. https://criticalRefugeestudies.com/resources/critical-vocabularies.

United Nations High Commissioner for Refugees (UNHCR). 1984. Cartagena Declaration on Refugees, Adopted by the Colloquium on the International Protection of Refugees in Central America, Mexico and Panama, Cartagena de Indias, Colombia. www.unhcr.org/en-us/about-us/background/45dc19084/cartagena-declaration-refugees-adopted-colloquium-international-protection.html.

———. 2002. "Guidelines on International Protection: Gender-Related Persecution within the Context of Article 1A(2) of the 1951 Convention and/or Its 1967 Protocol Relating to the Status of Refugees." www.unhcr.org/3d58ddef4.pdf.

———. 2011. The 1951 Convention Relating to the Status of Refugees and Its 1967 Protocol. www.unhcr.org/en-us/about-us/background/4ec262df9/1951-convention-relating-status-re%20fugees-its-1967-protocol.html.

———. 2016. "UNHCR's Views on Gender Based Asylum Claimsand Defining 'Particular Social Group' to Encompass Gender." www.unhcr.org/en-us/5822266c4.pdf.

———. 2018. Report of the United Nations High Commissioner for Refugees—Part II, Global Compact on Refugees. https://digitallibrary.un.org/record/1640526?ln=en#record-files-collapse-header.

———. 2020a. "Climate Change and Disaster Displacement." www.unhcr.org/en-us/climate-change-and-disasters.html.

———. 2020b. "Global Trends: Forced Displacement in 2019." www.unhcr.org/globaltrends2019/.

———. 2020c. "Figures at a Glance." www.unhcr.org/en-us/figures-at-a-glance.html.

———. 2021. "Which Countries Host the Most Refugees?" www.rescue.org/article/which-countries-host-most-refugees.

———. n.d. Convention Relating to the Status of Refugees. www.unhcr.org/4d934f5f9.pdf.

———. n.d. "Displacement in Central America." www.unhcr.org/en-us/displacement-in-central-america.html.

———. n.d. "Refugees and Asylum Seekers in Turkey." www.unhcr.org/tr/en/refugees-and-asylum-seekers-in-turkey.

US Department of State. 2016. "Protracted Refugee Situations." https://2009-2017.state.gov/j/prm/policyissues/issues/protracted/index.htm.

Vang, Ma. 2016. "Rechronicling Histories: Toward a Hmong Feminist Perspective." In Claiming Place: On the Agency of Hmong Women, edited by Chia Youyee Vang, Faith Nibbs and Ma Vang, 28–55. Minneapolis: University of Minnesota Press.

———. 2021. *History on the Run: Secrecy, Fugitivity, and Hmong Refugee Epistemologies*. Durham, NC: Duke University Press.

Vang, Ma, and Kit Myers. 2020. "At the Intersection of U.S. Military Imperialism and Racism: Tou Thao's Complicity in the Police Murder of George Floyd and Hmong Americans' Refusal to be a U.S. Ally." *Gendai Shiso,* October.

Villagran, Lauren, Daniel Connolly, and Aaron Montes. 2019. "Asylum Seekers in U.S. Face Years of Waiting, Little Chance of Winning Their Cases." *USA Today,* September 23. www.usatoday.com/in-depth/news /nation/2019/09/23/immigration-court-asylum-seekers-what-to-expect/2026541001/.

Visweswaran, Kamala. 1994. *Fictions of Feminist Ethnography.* Minneapolis: University of Minnesota Press.

Vuong, Ocean. 2019. *On Earth We're Briefly Gorgeous.* New York: Penguin Group.

Vo Dang, Thuy. 2005. "The Cultural Work of Anticommunism in the San Diego Vietnamese American Community." *Amerasia Journal* 31 (2): 65–86.

Volpp, Leti. 2015. "The Indigenous as Alien." *UC Irvine Law Review* 5 (2): 289–326.

Wamariya, Clemantine. 2019. *The Girl Who Smiled Beads.* New York: Broadway Books.

Wasko, Janet. 2014. "The Study of the Political Economy of the Media in the 21st Century." *International Journal of Media and Cultural Politics* 10 (3): 259–71.

Welna, David. 2020. "Coronavirus Has Now Killed More Americans than the Vietnam War." NPR, April 28. Accessed July 20, 2020. www.npr.org /sections/coronavirus-live-updates/2020/04/28/846701304/pandemic-death-toll-in-u-s-now-exceeds-vietnam-wars-u-s-fatalities

White, Melissa Autumn. 2014. "Documenting the Undocumented: Toward a Queer Politics of No Borders." *Sexualities* 17 (8): 980.

Willis, Emily Regan. 2019. "Alan Kurdi's Body on the Shore." In *Unwatchable,* edited by N. Baer, M. Hennefeld, and L. Horak et al., 102–7. New Brunswick, NJ: Rutgers University Press.

Wood, Nicholas. 2004. "A Fake Macedonia Terror Tale That Led to Deaths." *New York Times,* May 17. www.nytimes.com/2004/05/17/world/a-fake-macedonia-terror-tale-that-led-to-deaths.html.

Wright, Terence. 2002. "Moving Images: The Media Representation of Refugees." *Visual Studies* 17 (1): 53–66.

Yang, Boonmee. 2017. "the reason we indent." *MAI: Places We Came From, Places We Will Go* 2: 6.

Yue, Audrey. 2008. "Same-Sex Migration in Australia: From Interdependency to Intimacy." *GLQ: A Journal of Lesbian & Gay Studies* 14 (2–3): 239–62.

Index

www.ingramcontent.com/pod-product-compliance
Ingram Content Group UK Ltd.
Pitfield, Milton Keynes, MK11 3LW, UK
UKHW042053090325
456014UK00003B/53